TORRE DAVID
INFORMAL VERTICAL COMMUNITIES

For and because of Caracas

TORRE DAVID

INFORMAL VERTICAL COMMUNITIES

ALFREDO BRILLEMBOURG & HUBERT KLUMPNER
URBAN-THINK TANK
CHAIR OF ARCHITECTURE AND URBAN DESIGN
ETH ZÜRICH

PHOTOGRAPHS BY IWAN BAAN

LARS MÜLLER PUBLISHERS

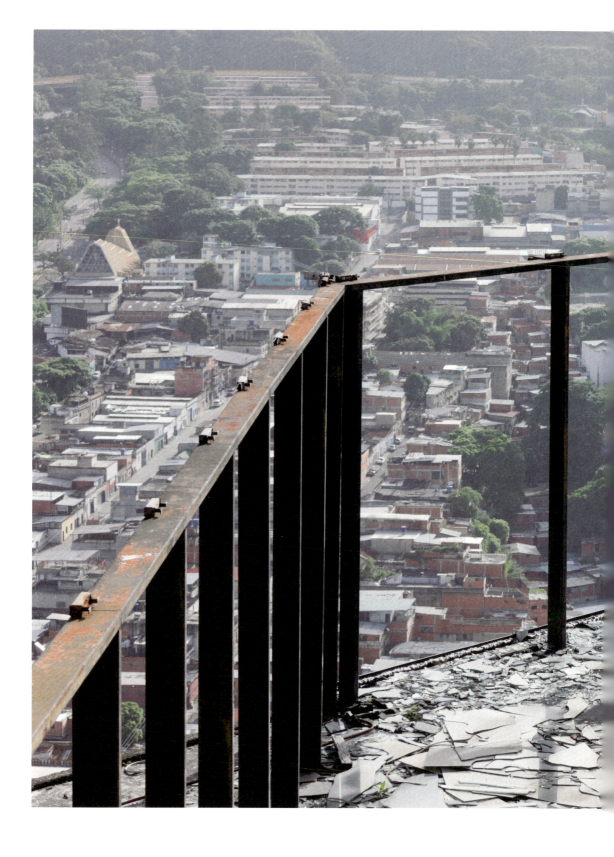

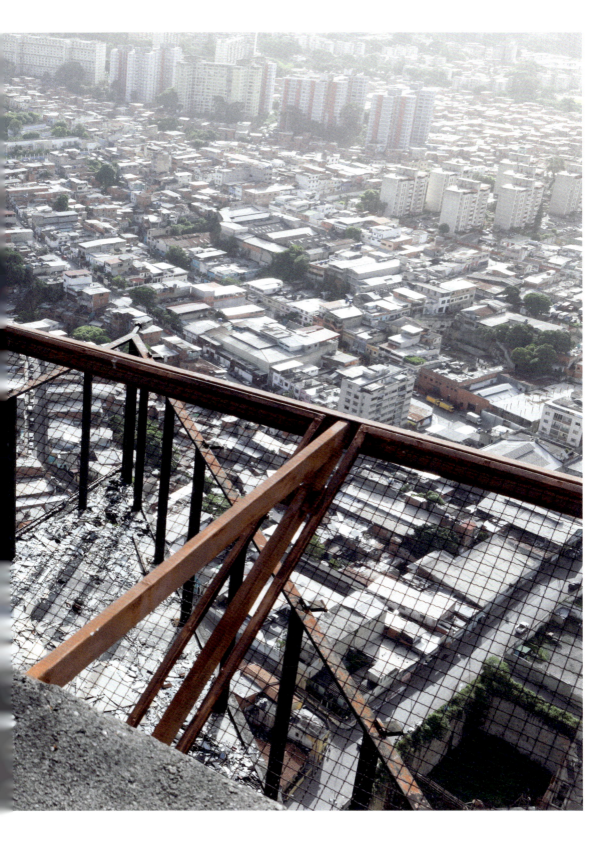

"The problem is not architecture.
The problem is the reorganization
of things which already exist."
—Yona Friedman

PREFACE

In one way or another, the third tallest building in Venezuela has been under construction for over twenty-one years. While Torre David (formerly known as the Centro Financiero Confinanzas) stands at an impressive 45 floors in the heart of Caracas' former central business district, it is unlikely that the building will ever be finished—at least not in the conventional sense. After the developer, David Brillembourg, passed away in 1993 and the financial group supporting the construction collapsed in the wake of the 1994 Venezuelan banking crisis, the tower was abandoned and became a magnet for squatters. Today, it is the improvised, continually revised home for more than 750 families living as a self-organized community in what some have called a vertical slum. That this community has not been riven by the contradictory and potent forces that surround and impinge upon it—that its members have, with great ingenuity and determination, turned a ruin into a home, albeit a precarious and marginal one—is nothing short of astonishing.

It is critically important that the research we undertook in Torre David, our observations about its physical and social dimensions, and our conclusions about its significance be placed in context:

As we hope this book makes abundantly clear, our focus here—as it has been in the other informal settlements Urban-Think Tank (U-TT) has engaged with—is not political, though it is impossible not to touch upon politics. We are not ideologues; we do not subscribe to any "-ism," either political or, for that matter, architectural. Our concern is the ethical and moral role of the architect in society, any society, regardless of its government. We believe that the architect's responsibilities precede and supersede any political system.

Indeed, we have lost faith—if, in fact, we ever had it—in the capacity and the will of any government to resolve the disparity between rich and poor, to recognize the value of a common ground, to blur the boundaries that divide the world into us and them, have and have-not. Instead, we put our faith for the realization of practical, sustainable solutions in the architectural profession; our colleagues in engineering and urban planning and design; in private enterprise and industry; and in the vast global population of slum-dwellers.

We neither support nor denounce invasions and squatter settlements. Whether or not they ought to have occurred is irrelevant to our work. We are concerned with what is. That the work of Enrique Gómez, one of Venezuela's most prominent architects and the designer of Torre David, was not fully realized and has, in the end, been all but obliterated, is nothing to be celebrated. But this is a fact. And it is in the past.

As much as we devote time and research to the origins of Torre David, it is to help us—and, we hope, our readers—understand how universal the issues are and how this tower came to be what it is today. In the end, how it came to be and who is responsible is far less important that its potential for pointing the way toward the future.

At U-TT, we have spent the last ten years seeking to understand how to improve the lives of under-served, often ill-served, city dwellers. We began with Caracas and its messy, complex, and tumultuous barrios and have since been working throughout the world, in mega-cities where the informal is rapidly taking over from the formal, traditional city. While we conduct interdisciplinary research both independently and through major educational institutions, U-TT is a design firm, building real projects that address many of the environmental challenges facing urban residents.

We believe that design—whether of buildings, public parks, or infrastructure— is an invaluable tool for improving lives. Torre David, with its magnificent deficiencies and remarkable assets, gives us the opportunity to consider how we can create and foster urban communities. Thus this book's discussion of our engagement with Torre David is intended as a call to action to our fellow architects, and all those who hope to become architects, to see in the informal settlements of the world the potential for innovation and experimentation, and to put their design talents in service to a more equitable and sustainable future.

Alfredo Brillembourg & Hubert Klumpner
Co-founders and co-principals of Urban-Think Tank
Chair of Architecture and Urban Design, ETH Zürich

INTRODUCTION:
AN URBAN EXPERIMENT
WITH THREE THOUSAND PARTICIPANTS

Andres Lepik

The spectacular tale of the unfinished Torre David high-rise in Caracas—originally a commercial development, but occupied by squatters since 2007—has begun to draw international attention.[1] Media interest tends to focus primarily on portraying a squalid world of poverty, violence, and danger in this "vertical slum," illustrated by individual tragedies, lurid images, and selective interviews. Against the backdrop of the political and social climate in Venezuela under Hugo Chávez's presidency, such stories are eagerly touted as metaphors for the country's overall situation. When the tower was stormed in April 2012 by security forces amidst suspicions (which later turned out to be unfounded) that a high-profile hostage was being held there, news of the incident associated the approximately 3,000 residents collectively with the criminal underworld.[2]

Slums, favelas, barrios—public awareness of the problems of informal settlements has been sharply heightened in recent years by popular books and films,[3] while contemporary artists such as JR have created headline-grabbing projects that further highlight the topic in the media.[4] At the same time, this increasing interest in the kind of slum conditions that have previously remained hidden from the public gaze has also prompted criticism of the commercial exploitation—"slum voyeurism" (Fareed Zakaria), even "poverty porn"—of such impoverished lives. What tends to be overlooked in most popular reporting of the issue is a deeper analysis of the specific underlying problems in each situation. Detailed research into the social, economic, technical, urban, and human elements, which this book presents in the context of Torre David, clearly indicates that the occupation of this high-rise represents a complex social experiment, the outcome of which is as yet unknown.
In the meantime, there are three specific questions we can address:
– Is Torre David—as is so often claimed—really a "vertical slum"?[5]
– How does Torre David compare with historical precedents, particularly with the squatters in Europe in the 1970s and 1980s?
– Does Torre David offer a model for the use of empty buildings in other countries?

1 Among the media covering Torre David recently are *Der Spiegel,* the *New York Times,* the BBC, and *Domus.*
2 See Chapter One, p. 100.
3 See Mike Davis, *Planet of Slums* (2006); Robert Neuwirth, *Shadow Cities* (2004); or Doug Saunders, *Arrival City* (2012); and such films as *City of God* and *Slumdog Millionaire.*

4 For example, JR's project, *Women are Heroes* (2008–2010), published in multiple magazines worldwide. See http://www.jr-art.net/projects.
5 Cf. Peter Wilson, "The Skyscraper Slums of Caracas," *Foreign Policy,* January 6, 2012, http://www.foreignpolicy. com/articles/2012/01/06/skyscraper_slum_caracas. The article also gives other examples in Caracas.

IS TORRE DAVID, IN FACT, A SLUM AT ALL?

It is somewhat difficult to define the term "slum." The current definition according to UN-HABITAT is based primarily on the lack of certain amenities, such as "durable housing of a permanent nature that protects against extreme climate conditions."[6] This first point alone does not apply to the current situation of most residents of Torre David because they are largely sheltered from the elements by the existing structure as well as by the walls they have built themselves. The arguments that follow—lack of access to water and sanitary facilities—do not apply either, as most residents do have water connections (albeit in regulated quantities) and their own toilets. At most, the last argument in the UN list, which specifies "security of tenure that prevents forced evictions," would be pertinent to the circumstances in Torre David, since the residents have received no formal recognition from the owners—the *Fondo de Garantía de Depósitos y Protección Bancaria* (FOGADE). Another indication of a slum situation, according to UN-HABITAT, is "overcrowding," which is defined as three or more persons sharing one room. While some spaces in Torre David do fit this last criterion, other apartments are spacious and afford individuals a degree of privacy.

In addition to those arguments, however, there are other soft factors that identify slums. These include a lack of access to public transport, which is often a major problem for people in informal settlements on the outskirts of cities. The relatively central location of Torre David makes access almost ideal. Another factor often mentioned is the lack of hygiene and safety in slums. Again, an analysis of the current situation in Torre David renders this argument moot: the residents appear to have created a highly efficient system of self-organization on each floor to ensure regular cleaning as well as sharing payment for electricity supply. Community groups addressing issues and initiatives on each floor attest to the high quality of the organizational structures that have been established here. Most floors are able to lock stairwell entrances, ensuring a good degree of social control from floor to floor, while community guards ensure surveillance of the main entrance—a feature normally associated with gated communities where the well-off isolate themselves for safety and security. As such a measure is usually intended to exclude people from lower social strata, the term "slum" hardly seems an appropriate description of the situation in Torre David. By comparison to such (in)famous slums as Dharavi in Mumbai or Kibera in Nairobi, there are simply too many "slum" criteria that do not apply here.

6 UN-HABITAT definition: http://www.unhabitat.org/
documents/media_centre/sowcr2006/SOWCR%205.pdf.

EUROPEAN SQUATTERS AS PRECEDENT?

One key criterion that does apply to Torre David is that the people who have moved in have no security of tenure. The current residents have taken control of the building without the permission of FOGADE and their occupancy is not assured, but merely temporarily tolerated. Whereas slums usually sprawl out across undeveloped areas on the outskirts of a city or on extremely unattractive sites within the city, Torre David is an existing architectural structure in a prime location with ample floor space that has been converted to residential use. In this respect, it appears to be a variation on the organized squats that were created in the 1970s and 1980s in Europe. Many of the squats in Europe (especially in Germany, Switzerland, and the Netherlands) were the product of a backlash against the widespread housing shortage that affected mainly low-income sectors of the population and were often initiated with explicitly political aims. In Caracas, too, there has been a dramatic decline in available housing, leading to a huge increase in informal settlements, or barrios. Unlike the squatters in Europe, most of the people here are not actually in opposition to the government; their occupation is a pragmatic self-help solution, rather than a protest. The long-term, strategic approach, however, is similar: the aim to establish a strong social network within the housing community

Dharavi, Mumbai, 2010.

Photo: U-TT/Ilana Millner

A squatted building in Berlin, 2009.

Photo: Thom Quine

and to project a strong sense of identity to the outside world. Acting together as a group, the residents have far more political clout than they would have as individuals. Many of the European squats were tolerated over a period of several years and some even ended up being permanently legalized by tenancy contracts. A similar principle can be seen at work in Torre David, where the residents fulfill the same obligations as legal occupants by paying their electricity bills to the local authorities, thereby gradually working towards recognition and legalization. In doing so, they appear to be giving the authorities as few grounds as possible to accuse them of breaking the law.

An interesting case for comparison is the community of Christiania in Copenhagen: what began there as the spontaneous occupation of some empty buildings on a former military site in the early 1970s burgeoned into a flourishing colony of people seeking an alternative lifestyle, until it eventually achieved legal recognition as an autonomous community (where even open trading in soft drugs was permitted). In Christiania, a handful of pioneers and rebels triggered a social dynamic that ultimately resulted in the formation of a parallel society within the existing urban fabric and, in turn, ended up becoming a tourist attraction in its own right. The political leverage that was accrued over time—toleration of the squatters by the authorities, their self-determined economic and social structures, and the community's increasing acceptance by the rest of the city—was used to achieve increasingly ambitious aims. Only recently, the 850 or so residents of Christiania, after lengthy negotiation with the municipal authorities, won the right to purchase the entire site.[7] Given its history so far, Torre David could well develop in a similar direction and become an autonomous zone within the city of Caracas. Its degree of self-organization and its various business models (from transport services to informal shops selling goods) have already created an economic framework that far surpasses the provisional nature of temporarily occupied buildings. Here, too, the large number of residents and the growing sense of community—including the now legally recognized in-house Asociacion Cooperativa de Vivienda "Casiques de Venezuela," R.L.—together with the length of time that the authorities have tolerated the occupation, will make it increasingly difficult for the government to find socially acceptable grounds for resettlement.

CAN TORRE DAVID BE A MODEL FOR OTHER PLACES?

Whether the Torre David model can be applied elsewhere is a question of topical importance, especially in light of the increasing public interest in issues surrounding the conversion and adaptive reuse of existing buildings in industrialized nations. At the 12th International Architecture Exhibition – la

7 See Reinhard Wolff, "Bewohner kaufen ihren Freistaat," *taz.de*, May 1, 2012, http://www.taz.de/!69970/.

Biennale di Venezia in 2010, the Dutch contribution focused on empty build-ings, under the motto *Vacant NL, Where Architecture Meets Ideas*[8] and charted the incidence of such buildings in a related art project with the title *Dutch Atlas of Vacancy.* The German contribution at the 2012 Biennale di Venezia ad-dressed a similar theme, under the motto *Reuse, Reduce, Recycle,* exploring the potential conversion and use of existing stock, while the Berlin-based internet platform *Leerstandsmelder* has begun identifying and mapping all the city's vacant buildings and inviting citizens to get involved in debating possible new uses for them.[9] Empty buildings are (once again) becoming a po-litical issue for which the broader public has to be mobilized if they want to have a say in urban planning and development.[10] In Europe, the debate about vacant buildings is set against the backdrop of a potentially dwindling popu-lation, first highlighted by the 2004/2005 exhibition *Shrinking Cities.*[11] As such, the issue in highly developed countries is framed by the question of whether, and to what extent, new buildings can be justified socially, ecologically, and economically.

Interestingly, the discussions triggered by these exhibitions and the pub-lications accompanying them were instigated by architects, who thereby ques-tioned their own accepted and familiar role in society. After all, it is architects who profit from any building boom, whereas they are likely to receive far lower fees for conversions and refurbishments. In order to understand the current situation a little better, it is necessary to explore the historic origins of the occupation of empty spaces.

The classic history of architecture usually starts with the idea of the primitive hut as the first building and goes on to describe the development of the discipline as an increasingly complex evolution of built structures. What tends to fall by the wayside in this narrative, however, is that other anthropo-logical constant that stems from the earliest humans seeking shelter from the elements in existing natural caves and spaces, which they would then use as dwelling places for a certain period. To the trained architect who earns a living designing buildings, the notion of appropriating spaces to live in must seem an undesirable departure from the "right path," because it requires no intel-lectual input in terms of concept and production. Cave dwelling has been re-garded since classical antiquity as a particularly primitive form of housing, earning entire tribes the derogatory epithet "troglodyte." Yet the appropriation and occupation of naturally occurring spaces as dwellings is a very obvious and economical choice. It brings to mind Diogenes, the ascetic philosopher who is said to have lived in a wooden barrel. Whether or not that is actually true, it does illustrate his eschewal of all superfluous things in life, as record-ed by multiple sources of the time. This asceticism included his dwelling. It

8 See Netherlands Architecture Institute, http://en.nai.nl/ museum/exhibitions/exhibition_archive/2011/item/_rp_ kolom2-1_elementId/1_770971.
9 See www.leerstandsmelder.de.
10 www.freespaceberlin.org explicitly notes properties in Berlin owned by the public sector.
11 For details of this research and exhibition project, see www.shrinkingcities.com.

is said that Diogenes would point to the Stoa of Zeus and the Pompeion and declare that Athens had provided him with excellent homes.[12] He used the public buildings constructed by the Athenians to live and sleep in because they were freely accessible and offered plenty of space. By assuming the right of the individual to make use of existing structures erected by the community, he provided the theoretical groundwork for all squatters.

The current residents of Torre David seized the opportunity of appropriating an existing structure, originally intended for a different purpose, and are using it to meet their urgent housing needs, gradually adapting it to meet certain standards of habitation. In the course of this experiment, the community of residents has become increasingly stable, creating autonomous organizational forms that reinforce their sense of identity and solidarity. The issue of legality remains unsolved, but the solidarity of the community and its increasing recognition indicate that their hopes of long-term acceptance may not be entirely unfounded.

12 Diogenes Laërtius, *Lives of Eminent Philosophers*, vol. 2, trans. Robert Drew Hicks (Cambridge, MA: Harvard University Press, 1970); see also Diogenes Laërtius, *Diogenes the Cynic: Sayings and Anecdotes*, trans. Robin Hard (New York: Oxford University Press, 2012), 10.

I wish to thank Alfredo Brillembourg and Hubert Klumpner for inviting me to visit Torre David with them in March 2012. This book marks what is undoubtedly one of the most unforgettable and unusual architectural experiences of my career to date.

The informal city stretches like fingers, reaching
towards the urban center of Caracas. The river
and highways demarcate a clear division between
where the formal city ends and the barrios begin.

Around 60 percent of Caracas' population lives
in the barrios, covering less than 40 percent of
the city's occupied land.

The partially finished Torre David is the third tallest building in Venezuela. Visible here are four of the five structures that compose the Torre David complex: Edificios A, B, K, and the parking garage. Not visible in this photograph is the atrium.

To allow for fresh air and natural light, some of
the residents of Edificio A have removed portions
of the glass façade.

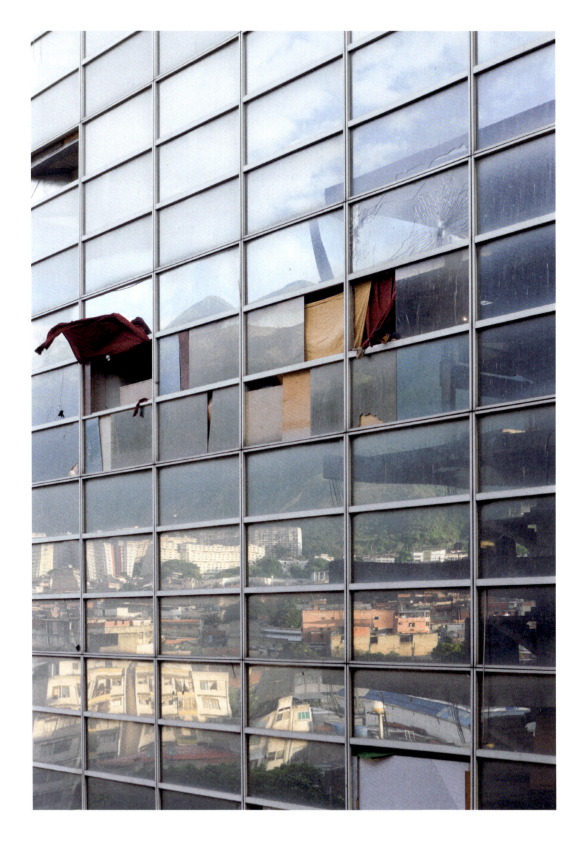

The story of Torre David is a tangle of history and human ingenuity, one that has unfolded over decades. Depicting its full scope and complexity in this book is impossible, but we have tried in the best way we know how: through an amalgamation of various modes of visualizing urban situations and their stories. As such, we teamed up with André Kitagawa, a Brazilian illustrator whose work often deals with the brutal, basic elements of modern cities. Educated as an architect, André inherently understood our interest in the Tower, as well as our need to convey the story in a way that adds a different sense of reality to the reader's perception of the site and community. André's keen eye for architecture and his storytelling instincts have produced another glimpse into the rise, occupation, and possible future of Torre David.

TORRE
A GRAPHIC NOVELLA
BY ANDRE KITAGAWA
WITH URBAN-THINK TANK

CARACAS, VENEZUELA
APRIL 9, 2012, 3 PM

AFTER RECEIVING A TIP THAT A KIDNAPPED COSTA RICAN DIPLOMAT WAS BEING HELD INSIDE A SQUATTED HIGH-RISE, SECURITY FORCES RAIDED THE TOWER.

FLOOR BY FLOOR...

...ROOM BY ROOM...

...THEY SEARCHED TO NO AVAIL.

THE NEXT DAY, HE WAS FOUND ELSEWHERE IN CARACAS. HOWEVER, THE SEARCH BROUGHT ATTENTION TO THIS 45-STORY GIANT IN THE MIDDLE OF THE CITY.

ONCE DESTINED TO BECOME A BEACON OF LUXURY AND PROSPERITY, IT IS INSTEAD NOW CONSIDERED BY SOME TO BE THE TALLEST SQUAT IN THE WORLD. IT IS KNOWN TO ALL AS...

...TORRE DAVID

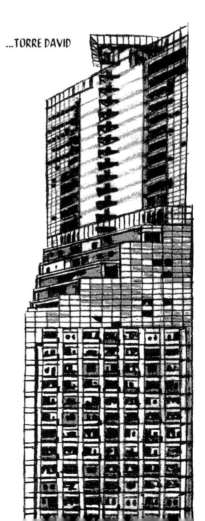

THIS IS THE CITY OF CARACAS, WHICH OVER THE PAST 60 YEARS EXPERIENCED EXTREME FORMAL AND INFORMAL GROWTH.

Barrio Petare

23 de Enero, 1958

23 de Enero, 2012

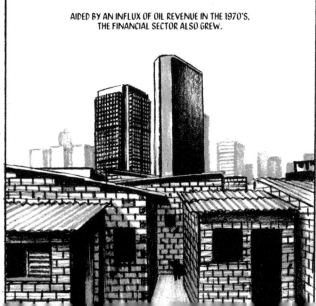

AIDED BY AN INFLUX OF OIL REVENUE IN THE 1970'S, THE FINANCIAL SECTOR ALSO GREW.

PROMINENT IN THIS EXPANSION WAS A DEVELOPER NAMED DAVID BRILLEMBOURG.

IN THE LATE 1980'S HE SET OUT TO BUILD A MASSIVE OFFICE AND COMMERCIAL COMPLEX, THE CENTRO FINANCIERO CONFINANZAS.

AT THE CENTER OF THIS COMPLEX WAS THE TORRE DAVID.

MEANWHILE, PRESIDENT CARLOS ANDRÉS PÉREZ RETURNED FOR A SECOND, DISASTROUS TERM.

MARKET REFORMS WENT AWRY AND MASSIVE SOCIAL UNREST ENSUED, NOW KNOWN AS THE CARACAZO.

CARACAS WAS SHAKEN, BUT LIFE WENT ON. DAVID BRILLEMBOURG BEGAN CONSTRUCTION OF THE COMPLEX IN 1990.

THE TOWER ROSE OVER THE COURSE OF ALMOST FOUR YEARS.

THEN TWO THINGS WENT TERRIBLY WRONG:

IN APRIL 1993, DAVID PASSED AWAY.

IN 1994 THE VENEZUELAN FINANCIAL SECTOR COLLAPSED AND THE FUNDING FOR CONSTRUCTION EVAPORATED.

90% COMPLETE, THE TOWER FELL UNDER GOVERNMENT OWNERSHIP.

AND SAT VACANT OVER THE NEXT 13 YEARS.

MEANWHILE, VENEZUELA EXPERIENCED MASSIVE POLITICAL CHANGE.
HUGO CHÁVEZ WAS ELECTED PRESIDENT...

...AND A NEW CONSTITUTION WAS WRITTEN.

CONSTITUCIÓN DE LA REPÚBLICA BOLIVARIANA DE VENEZUELA 1999

A SERIES OF LAWS AND PRESIDENTIAL DECREES UNDERMINED EXISTING VENEZUELAN PROPERTY LAW.

THE HOUSING SHORTAGE GREW MORE DIRE ALONG WITH POLITICAL AND ECONOMIC TROUBLES. PEOPLE BEGAN TO SQUAT PUBLIC AND PRIVATE SPACES ALL OVER THE COUNTRY.

ONE EVENING, IN SEPTEMBER 2007, AFTER DEVASTATING RAINFALL...

..FAMILIES FROM BARRIOS SURROUNDING THE CITY SET OUT TO FIND NEW SHELTER.

THEY DISCOVERED TORRE DAVID.

THOSE WHO ENTERED ON THE FIRST EVENING QUICKLY STAKED OUT SPACE ON THE GROUND FLOOR...

...AND SOON BEGAN EXPLORING THE REST OF THE TOWER.

AS MORE FAMILIES MOVED IN, THE INFORMAL INVASION GREW TO AN ORGANIZED OCCUPATION.

IN THE ABSENCE OF GOVERNMENT-SUPPORTED HOUSING, A COMMUNITY GREW THAT ADAPTED THE TOWER TO FIT ITS NEEDS.

TWO YEARS AFTER THE INVASION, THE RESIDENTS ESTABLISHED THE COOPERATIVE CASIQUES DE VENEZUELA.

Asociacion Cooperativa de Vivienda "Casiques de Venezuela"

A CHURCH WAS BUILT AND ATTRACTED A LARGE CONGREGATION.

RESIDENTS DEVISED THEIR OWN WASTE-DISPOSAL SYSTEMS, AND ORGANIZED THE STORAGE AND DISTRIBUTION OF WATER AND ELECTRICITY.

GROUPS WERE ORGANIZED TO GUARANTEE SECURITY AND MAINTENANCE.

GROCERY SHOPS...

...BARBERSHOPS AND A BASKETBALL COURT NATURALLY AROSE TO MEET THE NEEDS OF THE COMMUNITY

AFTER MANY UNCERTAINTIES, RESIDENTS BEGAN TO LOOK TOWARDS THE POSSIBILITY OF A BRIGHTER FUTURE.

MEANWHILE, ELSEWHERE IN CARACAS, URBAN-THINK TANK WAS WORKING IN THE BARRIOS AND FOLLOWING THE STORY OF TORRE DAVID.

AS CARAQUEÑOS THEMSELVES, THEY WERE INTERESTED IN WHAT WAS HAPPENING IN THE TOWER, AND WANTED TO FIND OUT MORE.

AFTER MANY MONTHS OF RESEARCH AND COLLABORATION IN THE TOWER, U-TT PRESENTED THEIR IDEAS AT A COMMUNITY MEETING.

DEAR FRIENDS...

...AFTER A YEAR AND A HALF OF DOCUMENTING THE STRUCTURE, INTERVIEWING MANY OF YOU, AND WORKING TOGETHER TO IDENTIFY KEY PROBLEMS...

...WE WANT TO DISCUSS SOME POSSIBLE RETROFITS FOR YOUR HOME.

WE WANT TO HELP YOU UPGRADE THE TORRE INTO IMPROVED SOCIAL HOUSING. LET US SHARE OUR VISION.

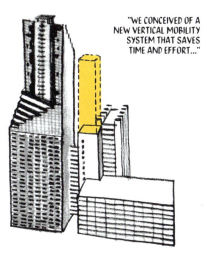

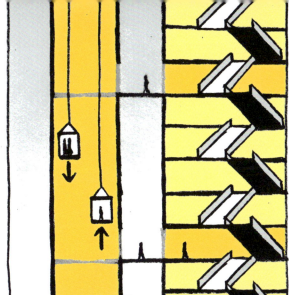

"WE CONCEIVED OF A NEW VERTICAL MOBILITY SYSTEM THAT SAVES TIME AND EFFORT..."

"...SUSTAINABLE ENERGY PRODUCTION AND STORAGE SYSTEMS..."

"...ADDITIONAL COMMERCIAL SPACES FOR RESIDENTS..."

"...NEW WATER SUPPLY INFRASTRUCTURE..."

"...FAÇADE IMPROVEMENTS..."

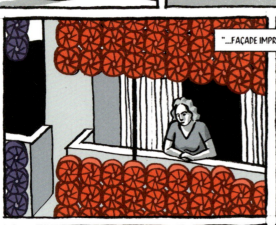

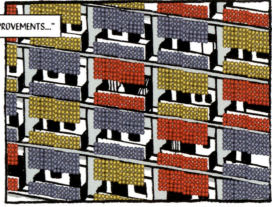

"...BETTER WASTE DISPOSAL CONDUITS..."

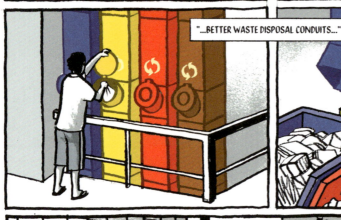

"...AND HYDROPONIC GARDENS..."

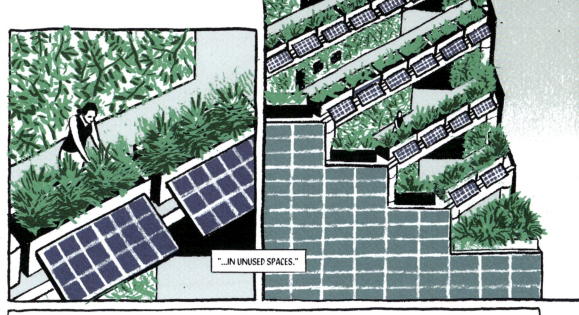

"...IN UNUSED SPACES."

"WE SEE TORRE DAVID AS A CATALYST FOR A NEW MODE OF URBAN DEVELOPMENT IN WHICH THE NEW CITY IS BUILT ON TOP OF THE OLD."

MOBILIZING THEIR TEAM OF RESEARCHERS AT ETH ZÜRICH, U-TT CONTINUES TO BUILD A BRIDGE BETWEEN TORRE DAVID AND FIRST WORLD INDUSTRY, ENABLING INNOVATIVE AND PRODUCTIVE COLLABORATION FOR BOTH.

TO BE CONTINUED...

"When we made the decision to occupy this space we found several realities, among them: this dead giant. A giant of 192 m, dead in the middle of our capital city, dead, with 45 floors uninhabited! When we arrived at the top floor of this tower and we stood on that heliport and we looked around, we realized that the whole population that had come to fill this land of Caracas—those who came from Los Llanos, from Colombia, from wherever they came from—we realized that not all of these people were here in the center, in the healthy, flat part of the city. All of these people were sent out, to the surroundings, to the hills, where there is a higher level of risk. They were told: go occupy those zones! And it was for this housing need that we deforested and damaged several spaces that today we know as our barrios."

—Fernando, former resident of Torre David

I: PAST

I came to myself in a dark wood
where the straight way was lost.[1]

It is 11:30 on a Thursday night, and some forty men and women are gathering in the unfinished lobby of an equally unfinished skyscraper, known as Torre David,[2] in the neighborhood of La Candelaria/San Bernardino, in the Libertador district of Caracas. The space, originally intended as a soaring atrium topped by a glass cupola, is open to the night sky and barely lit by fluorescent lights wired into corners and hanging from wall hooks. A recent storm has left puddles of water on the floor, and parked motorcycles tick quietly as they cool down.

The men and women are representatives of the residents of the skyscraper—"squatters" to some, "invaders" to others. They themselves prefer "neighbors." Some of the attendees are floor managers, others simply civic-minded.

The Tower's secretary and deputy manager of social services and finances is Gladys Flores, a petite 47-year-old woman with an air of authority. She calls the meeting to order; everyone stands, clasping hands for the customary opening prayer. Many of the residents are Evangelical Pentecostal Christians, their flock led by Alexander "el Niño" Daza, who is also president of the Tower cooperative. He delivers a passionate 20-minute sermon in which he asserts his conviction that Venezuelan president Hugo Chávez will, upon his inevitable reelection in October 2012, bless the residents with property rights. Other speakers, too, have politics on their minds: two floor managers explain how fellow residents can register as official members of the governing United Popular Social Party of Venezuela (PSUV); Fernando, a former resident and a long-time supporter of the Tower's occupation, is fed up with the government and expounds on the merits of anarchism.[3]

---

1 Dante Alighieri, *La Divina Commedia*, "Inferno" I. 2–3: *mi ritrovai per una selva oscura/ che la diritta via era smarrita*. Only in retrospect, with the aid of Virgil, does Dante come to understand just how he lost the "right" path and, eventually, finds salvation. It is no less important to understand how Caracas lost its way and by what means it might possibly recover.

2 The nomenclature surrounding this project can be confusing. The complex was originally named the Centro Financiero Confinanzas and consisted of a cluster of structures (see Chapter 2), of which the tall skyscraper was designated Edificio A. The latter has come to be called Torre David, after the developer, the late David Brillembourg, though that name is also a metonym for the complex.

Finally, under the wary gaze of the residents, a representative of an architectural and urban design firm rises to speak. He tells the group that his practice would like to work with the residents and to enlist the participation of the private sector, to help conceive, construct, and test various physical interventions and experimental prototypes, while documenting the ways in which the community has already transformed the Tower into their home.

How did the ruins of a postmodern skyscraper, conceived and launched with the corporate-capitalist optimism of the late 1980s and early 1990s, come to be the home to a 3000-person squatter community whose operating framework is social and its inclinations anarchist? How did Caracas lose its way? The answers begin—as do the answers to so many questions about contemporary Venezuela—in the country's vast petroleum deposits.

3 There is no small irony in Fernando's participation:
this passionate anarchist supporter of extra-legal invasions
is also a municipal employee, working for one of Caracas'
five mayors.

WEALTH & GROWTH

ORO NEGRO

Once Venezuela's first commercial oil well was drilled in 1914, petroleum sales quickly soared.[4] By 1925 oil surpassed coffee and cacao as the chief export;[5] just three years later, Venezuela led the world in crude oil extraction.[6] Forty years of relatively steady economic growth ensued, thanks to taxes on petroleum exports and the world's increasing demand. In 1960, Venezuela joined Iran, Iraq, Kuwait, and Saudi Arabia as a founding member of OPEC.

Although the price of Venezuelan crude had remained fairly stable through the 1950s and 1960s, the 1972 Arab-Israeli War radically changed the market, to the country's short-term benefit. When the Arab members of OPEC, joined by Egypt, Syria, and Tunisia, retaliated against America's support for Israel by imposing an oil embargo, Venezuela stepped into the breach, increasing its rate of production and export. In just one year, the price of Venezuelan light crude leapt by 200 percent, giving the first administration of Carlos Andrés Pérez a massive influx of wealth.[7]

Awash in oil profits, the government went on a spending spree. In just five years, from 1974 to 1979, it managed to spend more money than had all other Venezuelan governments over the previous 143 years combined,[8] investing heavily in social, educational, housing, sanitation, and transportation infrastructure programs.[9] Pérez's grand plan for making Caracas a truly global city seemed visionary, but it was a vision delimited by the dominant principles of the 1970s, notably centralized grand-scale planning, a concept that has since collapsed under its own weight. That utopian thinking bred Parque Central, a vast residential, business, and cultural complex, essentially an autonomous city. Even earlier, in the 1950s and 1960s, Caracas had already attracted world-renowned architectural and engineering talent, giving rise to the University City, by Carlos Raul Villanueva; private homes designed by the likes of Gio Ponti and Richard Neutra; and new architecture practices established by former students of Mies Van Der Rohe, Walter Gropius, and other modernist masters. For these luminaries, their clients, and their successors, Caracas became a laboratory for experimentation and a locus for the conflation of wealth and architectural innovation.

Centralization underlay the development of the Caracas metro, which connected the periphery—including the enormous barrios of Petare and 23 de Enero—to the heart of the city, with the unintended consequence of flooding the formal city with the informal, to the ultimate deterioration of the rational modernist vision. On the other hand, during Pérez's first term in office public

4 Michael H. Tarver and Julia C. Frederick, *The History of Venezuela* (Westport, CT: Greenwood Press, 2005), 82.

5 Steve Ellner, "Introduction: The Search for Explanations," in *Venezuelan Politics in the Chávez Era,* ed. Steve Ellner and Daniel Hellinger, (Boulder, CO: Lynne Rienner Publishers, Inc., 2003), 7–26.

6 Tarver and Frederick, *The History of Venezuela*, 15.

7 Ibid. Pérez benefited similarly from armed conflict—the so-called "Desert Storm"—in his second term, when the U.S. requested that Venezuela increase oil production to compensate for the interruption of flow from the Middle East.

8 Tarver and Frederick, *The History of Venezuela*, 125.

employment doubled,[10] and the Venezuelan people enjoyed a rapid and dramatic improvement in services and benefits.

Pérez's vision was not limited to the city of Caracas. On January 1, 1975, the government, hoping to increase exports of iron and steel products, nationalized the iron and aluminum industries. The construction of the Guri Dam—the world's third-largest hydroelectric dam—in 1978 gave considerable momentum to that industry. So, too, did Ciudad Guayana, a new modernist industrial center whose design and planning were led in the early 1960s by professionals from MIT and Harvard. But Ciudad Guayana has been plagued by the adverse social effects that are now understood to be common when such a development is located without regard to context, in the middle of nowhere. And while for its first two decades the dam brought relatively clean and abundant electricity to Caracas, the demand created by the city's rapid growth has since exceeded supply. The ever-increasing usage and the absence of maintenance and capital improvements—of the dam's four turbines, only two are operational—have lead to frequent power shortages and blackouts in the city.

The schemes of centralization and nationalization continued to dominate the government's agenda; in 1976, it nationalized all foreign oil companies doing business in Venezuela. That seemed a good idea: by 1980, the petroleum industry accounted for seventy percent of the nation's revenues.[11]

If something seems too good to be true, it probably is. Seduced and distracted by enormous wealth, many in the government, not least the president, failed to include in its expenditures payment of the country's quickly mounting debt, primarily the result of investment in the development of the iron, steel, and aluminum industries. Professor John V. Lombardi, a scholar of Latin American history and specialist in Venezuela, puts it succinctly:

> In an almost desperate cycle, the government shores up the export model to generate sufficient revenue to operate the bureaucracy and, with the revenue that remains, make progress on improving society and diversifying the export economy. The extractive engine ties the government almost completely to world market prices for Venezuelan commodities, and those fluctuate on short-term cycles. Consequently, the government has only a short time to do what it can before the price falls and a new cycle begins. It often borrows money to prolong or speed up progress, and in borrowing money becomes even more dependent on the extractive engine to generate the funds to pay the country's debts.[12]

9 John V. Lombardi, "Prologue: Venezuela's Permanent Dilemma," in *Venezuelan Politics in the Chávez Era,* ed. Steve Ellner and Daniel Hellinger, (Boulder, CO: Lynne Rienner Publishers, Inc. 2003), 1–6.
10 Tarver and Frederick, *The History of Venezuela,* 126.
11 Ibid., 125.
12 "Prologue: Venezuela's Permanent Dilemma," 1–6.

Avenida Urdaneta, Caracas, September 7, 1961.
The influx of oil wealth in Caracas contributed to the
growth of an automobile culture.

All photos: Archivo Fotográfico Shell-CIC UCAB

Avenida Urdaneta, Caracas, July 15, 1958.

Venezuelans grew happily accustomed to the steady increase in the quality of life and saw no downside to their dependence on the government for highly subsidized goods. Lulled into complacency by the past, content in the present, they were blindsided by the immediate future.

BLACK FRIDAY

High foreign debt, enormous internal and external pressure to pay off that debt, and policies that effectively drove revenue overseas: their first victim was the *bolívar* itself, long considered one of the most stable currencies in the world.[13] On February 28th, 1983, four years into his five-year term, President Luis Herrera Campíns devalued the bolívar—the first devaluation in forty years. The resulting inflation devastated the middle class, the value of whose savings was suddenly cut in half.

With what came to be known as Black Friday, Venezuela began its downward spiral into "not only a material but also an ideological crisis from which the country never recovered."[14] Throughout the 1980s, funding for social services decreased, and the middle class shrank significantly. Until that time, the generous infusion of oil money had, as Professor Patricia Márquez notes, "prevented serious social conflict by allowing the nation at least a superficial resolution of its many structural problems."[15]

Even in the shadow of Black Friday, there remained some optimists in Venezuela. In 1984, work started on several major construction projects: the West Tower of the Parque Central Complex, the Mercantil Tower, and the BBVA Banco Provincial Tower.

The crisis cost President Luis Herrera Campíns a second term, and, in February 1984, Jaime Lusinchi was inaugurated. Not quite four years later, a new devaluation of the bolívar drove higher levels of inflation. Lusinchi, not having proven the country's savior, lost out in early February, 1989, when Venezuelans, looking to the past to rescue the future, elected Pérez once more.

CARACAZO

In a remarkably short time, it became clear that Pérez was not the answer, either. Just fourteen days after taking office, he announced *el paquete económico,* an IMF-backed structural adjustment program. In compliance with that plan, Pérez freed interest rates and abandoned fixed exchange rates, "allowing the *bolívar* to lose almost two-thirds of its purchasing power against the dollar" within the first six months of his term.[16] Pérez also cut government

---

13 "The Weakening of the 'Strong Bolívar,'" *The Economist,* January 14, 2010, http://www.economist.com/node/15287355.
14 Daniel Hellinger, "Political Overview: The Breakdown of Puntofijismo and the Rise of Chavismo," in *Venezuelan Politics in the Chávez Era,* ed. Steve Ellner and Daniel Hellinger, (Boulder, CO: Lynne Rienner Publishers, Inc. 2003), 27–54.

15 Patricia Márquez, "The Hugo Chávez Phenomenon: What Do 'the People' Think?" in *Venezuelan Politics in the Chávez Era,* ed. Steve Ellner and Daniel Hellinger, (Boulder, CO: Lynne Rienner Publishers, Inc. 2003), 197–213.
16 James Brooke, "International Report; Latin America Pursues Recovery on 2 Fronts," *New York Times,* August 28, 1989, http://www.nytimes.com/1989/08/28/business/

subsidies and drew up a list of state companies to be sold to the private sector.[17] Massive inflation and a spike in unemployment rates resulted. One of the first measures to be enacted in the free-market shock treatment was the elimination of existing petroleum subsidies, announced over the weekend of February 25th and 26th.

Virtually overnight, petrol prices rose by 100 percent; the government responded by mandating a 30-percent increase in public transportation fares. As Margarita López Maya points out, the government's adoption of a neoliberal program of structural adjustment amounted to a shift from paternalism to laissez faire and "a betrayal of the moral economy."[18] The poor, who had come to think of the fruits of paternalism as their right, felt abandoned. For their part, Pérez's political associates felt betrayed and were quick to undermine both his efforts and his administration.

As students and workers began their Monday morning commute, they were met by public transportation drivers demanding fares in excess of the government-mandated increase. This direct assault on their wallets was too much for the already agitated riders. Students began a protest, which quickly absorbed the greater population. Left unchecked by limited police response and a delay in action by government officials, the protests escalated, accompanied by widespread looting and the blocking of main traffic arteries throughout Caracas and in cities across the country.[19]

President Pérez finally responded, 24 hours later, by instituting martial law, suspending certain elements of the constitution, and putting a strict 6pm-to-6am curfew into effect. Relative calm finally returned, but the price was high: the government put the official death toll at 287,[20] but estimates of the real number vary greatly—from just under 300 to 1,500—depending upon the source.

The protests were, in some respects, the least of the country's problems. Thanks to the economic reforms, Venezuela's "accumulated inflation reached an unprecedented 150 percent" between 1989 and 1991.[21] Economic and political vicissitudes schooled Venezuelans in a tough new economic reality: forget tomorrow—spend your money while it is still worth something.[22] That lesson took hold, and today Venezuela is still marked by a culture of spending, in which even barrio-dwellers invest in tangible goods, at the expense of savings.

The cost to the fabric of the city has continued to rise ever since. The process of centralization brought uncountable numbers of people from the countryside to Caracas in search of work. In just one decade, from 1971 to 1981, the total population of Caracas grew from 3.2 million to 4.8 million. Some estimates put the current population at closer to six million or more,

international-report-latin-america-pursues-recovery-on-2-fronts.html.

17 Ibid.

18 Margarita López Maya, "The Venezuelan *Caracazo* of 1989: Popular Protest and Institutional Weakness," *Journal of Latin American Studies* 35, no. 1 (Feb. 2003): 117–37, http://www.jstor.org/stable/3875580.

19 Ibid.

20 Hellinger, "Political Overview: The Breakdown of Puntofijismo and the Rise of Chavismo," 31.

21 Tarver and Frederick, *The History of Venezuela*, 140.

22 Lombardi, "Prologue: Venezuela's Permanent Dilemma," 3.

depending upon where one establishes the boundaries within which the count is taken.[23]

The city was unprepared for the multitudes and the violence and spun out of control. Its five semi-autonomous municipalities each established quasi-private police forces and created "secure zones," dividing the city into revolutionaries and reactionaries. The latter, having lost faith that any authority could protect them, fed a multi-billion-dollar industry of private security and gated enclaves whose walls were topped with barbed wire and glass shards. Contemporary Caracas is rated one of the most violent cities in the world; in 2011, there were 2,215 homicides within the Libertador Municipality alone.[24] It is also among the most fragmented cities in its politics, economy, culture, and urban fabric. Major roadways cut through the urban fabric, isolating communities from one another. Fearful for their safety, people gravitate to shopping malls, bubbles of civic life insulated from the violence of the streets.

23 Any census in Caracas—indeed, any attempt to count individuals in any circumstance—is always fraught with contingencies. No one has been able to establish definitively the population of the barrio of Petare, let alone that of the ring of hillside barrios.

24 "Caracas is the World's Third Most Violent Sub-National Jurisdiction," *El Universal* (Caracas), April 27, 2012, http://www.eluniversal.com/nacional-y-politica/120427/caracas-is-the-worlds-third-most-violent-sub-national-jurisdiction.

THE TOWER RISES

To some, however, the future of Caracas still seemed promising.

In January 1990, ground was broken in the Libertador Municipality of downtown Caracas for the Centro Financiero Confinanzas. Its location could not have been more advantageous:

Libertador lies in the western portion of Caracas, in the heart of the valley that holds the city. Located at the intersection of Calle Real de Sarría and Avenida Urdaneta, the Centro Confinanzas occupies a plot adjacent to the Mercantil Tower and diagonally across from the BBVA Banco Provincial Tower. The neighborhood boasts two grand landmarks: the Parque Central Complex, which features what were then the tallest concrete skyscrapers in South America; and El Ávila, the mountainous national park that looms over the city and separates it from the Caribbean Sea. Nearby is the Avenida Boyacá, an arterial road constructed in the 1970s that runs along the base of El Ávila. To the east sits the small Barrio Sarria, one of many pockets of informal urban growth scattered in and around the city.

A concentration of political and financial power, literal and symbolic, distinguishes the district: the presidential palace, federal legislative palace, public ministry, headquarters of the Central Bank of Venezuela, and some of the tallest of the city's skyscrapers. The area had become Caracas' Wall Street, the center of finance and the prime location for building the global city.

Even amid such wealth, the Centro Financiero Confinanzas was intended to stand out as the epitome of luxury and prosperity.

The man behind this vision was developer Jorge David Brillembourg Ortega,[25] a primary investor in the construction of the Centro Confinanzas, conceiving it as the largest private skyscaper complex in South America. In a recent interview with Urban-Think Tank, David Brillembourg Jr. explained that his father had built another tower in the neighborhood in 1983; ten years later he decided to purchase the site upon which he built Torre David—what he hoped would become the "financial nerve of the city."[26] David Brillembourg Sr. expected that, within four or five years, there would be a dearth of office space in Caracas and, anticipating high demand, planned to offer luxury offices and hotel space on prime real estate at the heart of Caracas' banking district. Joining David Brillembourg Sr. in that endeavor were his brother, René Brillembourg, who was instrumental in promoting the construction; Enrique Gómez, lead architect on the project, and Mathias Brewer of Brewer & Brewer, who led design and development; Frank Kelemen of Keleman & Keleman, responsible for construction programming; and

---

25 Cousin of the author, Alfredo Brillembourg.
26 David Brillembourg Jr., interviewed by Ilana Millner
and Daniel Schwartz, Caracas/Zurich, July 2, 2012.

EL PANTEÓN

EL SILENCIO

Page 82–83

A

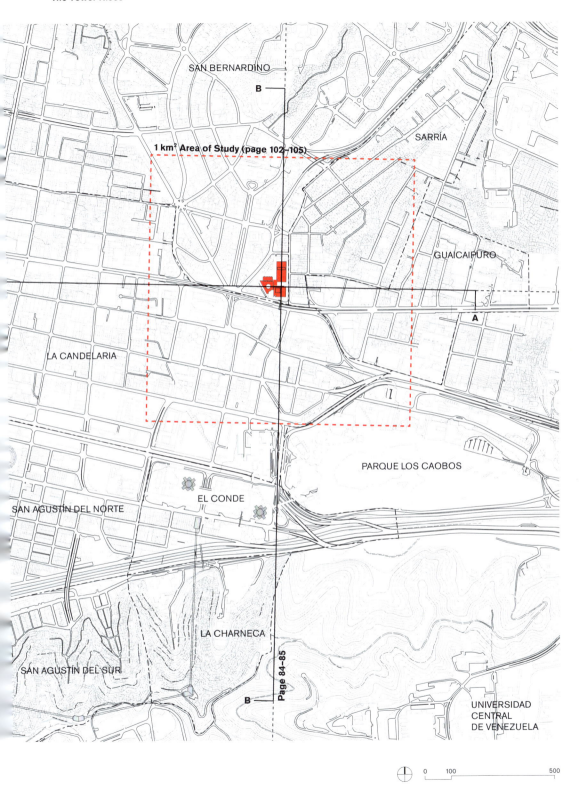

SAN BERNARDINO

B

SARRÍA

1 km² Area of Study (page 102–105)

GUAICAIPURO

A

LA CANDELARIA

PARQUE LOS CAOBOS

EL CONDE

SAN AGUSTÍN DEL NORTE

LA CHARNECA

SAN AGUSTÍN DEL SUR

B

Page 84–85

UNIVERSIDAD
CENTRAL
DE VENEZUELA

0   100   500

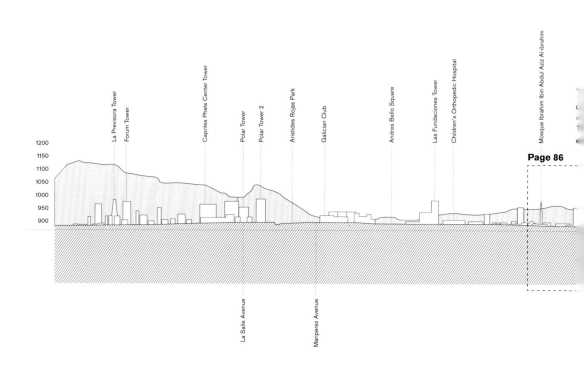

La Previsora Tower
Forum Tower
Capriles Pheis Center Tower
Polar Tower
Polar Tower 2
Aristides Rojas Park
Galician Club
Andres Bello Square
Las Fundaciones Tower
Children's Orthopedic Hospital
Mosque Ibrahim Ibin Abdul Aziz Ai-Ibrahim

Page 86

1200
1150
1100
1050
1000
950
900

La Salle Avenue

Mariperez Avenue

Sea Level

Site Section A-A

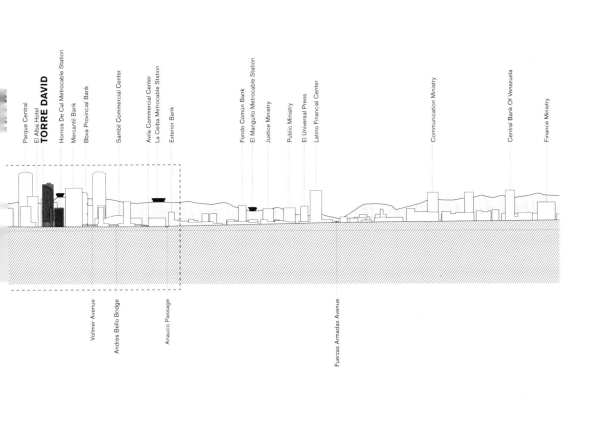

Parque Central
El Alba Hotel
TORRE DAVID
Hornos De Cal Metrocable Station
Mercantil Bank
Bbva Provincial Bank
Sambil Commercial Center
Avila Commercial Center
La Ceiba Metrocable Station
Exterior Bank
Fondo Comun Bank
El Manguito Metrocable Station
Justice Ministry
Public Ministry
El Universal Press
Latino Financial Center
Communication Ministry
Central Bank Of Venezuela
Finance Ministry

Vollmer Avenue
Andres Bello Bridge
Anauco Passage
Fuerzas Armadas Avenue

0   100

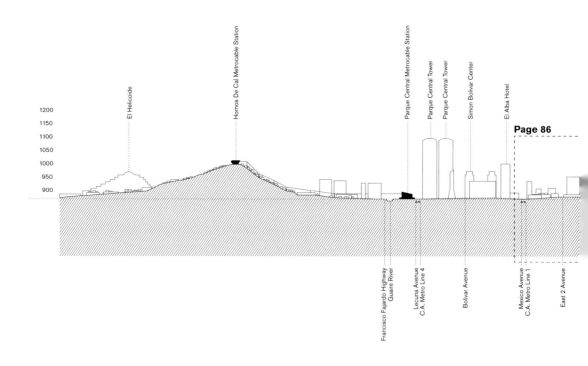

1200
1150
1100
1050
1000
950
900

El Helicoide

Hornos De Cal Metrocable Station

Parque Central Metrocable Station

Parque Central Tower

Parque Central Tower

Simon Bolivar Center

El Alba Hotel

Page 86

Francisco Fajardo Highway
Guaire River

Lecuna Avenue
C.A. Metro Line 4

Bolivar Avenue

Mexico Avenue
C.A. Metro Line 1

East 2 Avenue

Sea Level

Site Section B-B

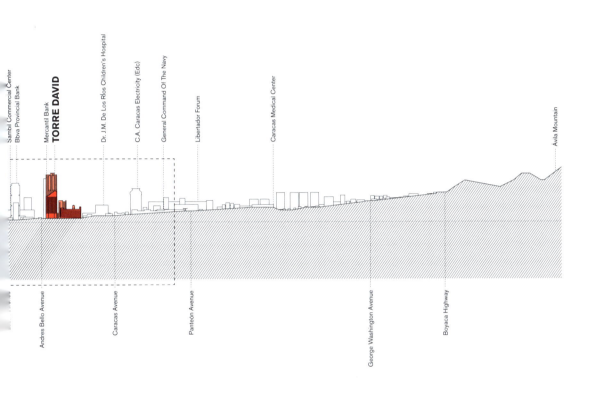

Sambil Commercial Center
Bbva Provincial Bank
Mercantil Bank
TORRE DAVID
Dr. J.M. De Los Ríos Children's Hospital
C.A. Caracas Electricity (Edc)
General Command Of The Navy
Libertador Forum
Caracas Medical Center
Avila Mountain

Andres Bello Avenue
Caracas Avenue
Panteón Avenue
George Washington Avenue
Boyaca Highway

0   100

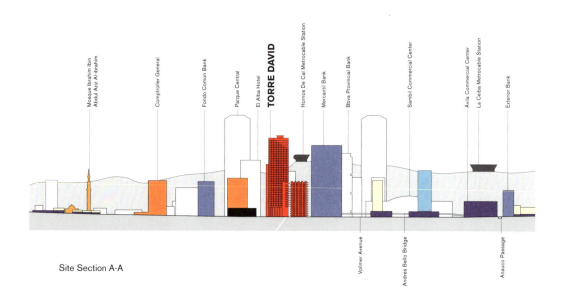

Site Section A-A

■ Occupations	■ Education
■ Government	■ Commercial
■ Religious	■ Bank
■ Housing	■ Office
■ Health	■ Parking

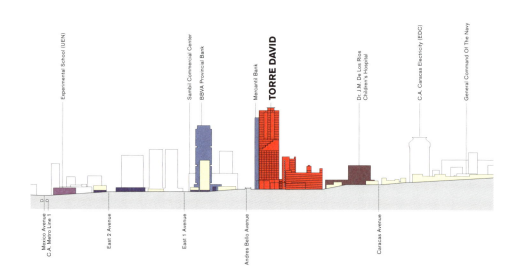

Site Section B-B

0   50

Tegaven, a Portuguese company specializing in concrete, serving as general contractor.[27]

THE PROGRAM

At any time, and in any place, the five concrete structures that comprised the Centro Confinanzas would have been ambitious. According to estimates given by René Brillembourg in a 1992 interview, the total cost of the complex was expected to reach 5,700 million *bolivarés*—the equivalent, at the time, of approximately US$82 million.[28] Edificio A (Torre David), the main building, was to top out at 45 stories, surmounted by a helipad. The first six floors were to house hotel support services; floors 7–16 were intended for the a hotel; floors 18–45 were planned for 30,000 m² of office space for the Confinanzas Group and the Banco Metropolitano de Crédito Urbano. The 17th floor was designed as a pressurized, hermetically sealed shelter for office workers, able to withstand four hours of intense heat from a possible fire. If the office floors were distinctly high-end, the hotel was *grande luxe:* its design called for no less than 21,000 m² of Italian marble; it would be protected with a state-of-the-art security system by Honeywell.[29]

Edificio B, planned as a 16-story structure, was to house 81 apartment suites for use by executives. A swimming pool on level 6 was to be accessible to hotel guests via a bridge connecting to Edificio A. A later addition to the plans, Edificio K, would be sandwiched between the other two, housing six elevators.

A large parking garage was essential to a massive complex in a car-oriented city; the Centro's 10-story parking garage was designed for an average of 890 vehicles—as many as 1,200 when parking attendants were employed.[30]

The atrium—the 30-m-high, 1,500 m²-heart of the complex—was to be capped by a glass dome and would feature elevators with panoramic city views, artwork by Baltazar Lobo,[31] and the hotel entrance. Altogether, the complex would be served by 23 Schindler-made elevators; eleven, exclusively for the office floors, would reach speeds of 5 m/sec.; those for the lower levels would reach speeds of up to 3.5 m/sec.

Even the less obviously magnificent elements of the project were on a grand scale. Halfway through its construction, Edificio A had already consumed 30,000 m³ of concrete, with estimates of up to 40,000 m³ for the balance of the complex.[32] Construction of all three towers was expected to require a total of 9,400 tons of steel. For the design and fabrication of the glass curtain wall, the developer selected Cupples Industries, famous for the façades of the Sears Tower, the John Hancock Center, the World Trade Center, and the Hong Kong

27 Carlos González Saavedra, "El Musmon Vuelve A La Carga: Confianza En Las Alturas," *Inmuebles* (Caracas), September 30, 1992, 10–18.

28 Ibid.

29 Ibid.

30 Ibid.

31 Enrique Gómez and Julio Rey, interviewed by Rafael Machado and Mathieu Quillici, Caracas, February 15, 2012. Enrique Gómez was the Centro Financiero Confinanzas project architect, and Julio Rey was an intern in Gómez's office at the time of construction.

32 González Saavedra, "El Musmon Vuelve A La Carga: Confianza En Las Alturas," 10–18.

and Shanghai Bank Corporation Towers. The hermetically sealed façade of Edificio A alone called for 30,000 m² of glass curtain wall, even though the north and south façades were covered in honeycombed aluminum panels for greater durability and resistance to the elements.[33]

As construction proceeded, additions and alterations were made to the design—not only the insertion of Edificio K, but also the addition of three floors to Edificio B, and at David Brillembourg's personal insistence, the creation of a rooftop helipad. He envisioned the helipad both as a further means of emergency egress and in the belief that helicopter transport would become popular in Caracas, as it had in São Paolo, for avoiding traffic and ensuring greater security.

The Caracas government, too, was caught up in the fervor of development. Architect Enrique Gómez was collaborating with Metro de Caracas C.A. to redesign the entire urban fabric of the area surrounding the Centro Financiero. As part of this scheme, the North-South avenues were to be moved underground, an endeavor financed by the banks in the Libertador Municipality, in coordination with the mayor.[34]

For almost four years, the complex gradually emerged from the ground, Edificio A rising to meet its skyscraper neighbors. The scheduled completion was July 1994, with the grand opening of the hotel planned for December of that year.

Then things went terribly wrong, beginning with the April, 1993 death from natural causes of David Brillembourg, just 55 years old.

STRUCTURALLY SOUND, FINANCIALLY CRIPPLED

Perhaps Brillembourg's brother could have picked up the reins, aided by the design and construction team, had it not been for a far greater crisis: in January 1994, Venezuela was hit by a series of bank closures that brought the financial sector to its knees.

First to collapse was Banco Latino, Venezuela's second-largest bank at the time. Over the course of the year, "more than half of the country's 47 commercial banks had become candidates for a bail-out by the state deposit-guarantee agency."[35] David Brillembourg's financial arm, Grupo Confinanzas, had been supported by a number of banks. It, too, failed. Without leadership or funds to continue construction, the project was almost immediately abandoned, leaving Edificio A, by Enrique Gómez's estimate, 90 percent complete.

David Brillembourg's tower aptly illustrates the law of unintended consequences, his project's rise and demise intimately connected to the boom-

---

33 Ibid.
34 Gómez and Rey, Feburary 15, 2012.
35 "Chaos in Caracas," *The Economist*, April 10, 1997,
http://www.economist.com/node/1044426.

and-bust cycle of politics and the economy in Venezuela. As Steve Ellner points out, "[p]rior to 1989, Venezuela was Latin America's 'near perfect' democracy";[36] Brillembourg's push for the Centro Confinanzas was conceived during the final years of relative stability and prosperity, and enacted during the first spasms of the radical change and political turmoil of the 1990s.

FOGADE

After the failure of the banks within Grupo Confinanzas, FOGADE *(Fondo de Garantía de Depósitos y Protección Bancaria)* seized the assets of Brillembourg's financial group and took over the Centro Confinanzas, which had come to be known as Torre David. Affiliated with the People's Ministry of Planning and Finance, FOGADE is responsible for insuring public deposits held in banks, savings and loan institutions, and other institutions in Venezuela.[37] FOGADE can also act to liquidate banks and their related companies.[38]

In FOGADE's hands, Torre David sat vacant for over 12 years. In 2001, FOGADE put the complex up for auction, valuing it at US$60 million. There were no takers. According to David Brillembourg Jr., when FOGADE finally brought the complex to market, "the window for doing something, which was two or three years later—almost immediately—had passed. After five or six years, it was a time when people weren't interested in finishing [the project]. Caracas had changed, Venezuela had changed."[39] As of September 2012, the complex has yet to be sold.

Periodic invasions of squatters and looters picked over abandoned machinery, construction materials, and large glass windows in Torre David, selling off whatever they could salvage. In the heart of a struggling financial district, the Tower stood dark and silent—a sad relic of the hopes and ambitions harbored by Venezuelans in the 1970s and early 1980s, and an inescapable reminder of the economic upheavals that followed those boom years.

36 Ellner, "Introduction: The Search for Explanations," 7–26.
37 Fondo de Protección Social de los Depósitos Bancarios (FOGADE). "Objetivo." Gobierno Bolivariano de Venezuela. Accessed July 27, 2012. http://fogade.gob.ve/Objetivos/Objetivos.htm.
38 Ibid.
39 David Brillembourg Jr., July 2, 2012.

INMUEBLES

CARACAS · 30 DE SEPTIEMBRE 1992　　AÑO 1 · Nº 3　Bs. 150

CONFIANZA EN LAS ALTURAS
Alarde de innovaciones en el mayor complejo de Latinoamérica

Es militar la administradora más grande del país

¿Sobreoferta en el mercado de oficinas?

Dos testigos del Renacimiento cultural mexicano

MERCADOS:
LITORAL CENTRAL • PUERTO PIRITU

Foto: Pineda - Lorenzo

All photos: Inmuebles Magazine/Pineda y Lorenzo

CONSTRUCCION

Images from a feature article on the Centro Financiero
Confinanzas, published in *Inmuebles* magazine's
September 1992 edition.

All photos: Inmuebles Magazine/Pineda y Lorenzo

POLITICAL FOMENT, LEGAL FICTION

With the economy well and truly disabled, it was the turn of the body politic to run amok. At the epicenter of a decade's-worth of convulsions was Hugo Chávez Frías, the beginning of whose ascent to power coincided with the construction of Torre David. Midway through that effort, on February 4, 1992, Chávez and a band of fellow military officers from the Movimiento Bolivariano Revolucionario 200 (MBR-200)[40] staged a short-lived coup. Failing to capture President Pérez and to secure the Miraflores presidential palace, Chávez nonetheless captured the attention of the public.

The uprising was crushed and Chávez went to jail, although not before announcing to the public that, in so many words, his fight was far from finished. Indeed, three years after his 1994 release, Chávez and his supporters formed their own political party, the Fifth Republic Movement (MVR), to campaign for Chávez's election. Their efforts culminated in his victory on December 6, 1998, an occasion that made apparent the "popular rejection of the two-party system"[41] and established Chávez as a "symbol of the opposition to the 1958 Venezuelan political model."[42] Chávez responded to the previous neoliberal reforms of both Pérez and Caldera's second terms in office with an evolving doctrine of populist liberation. He was inaugurated on February 2, 1999.

In the years since, a perfect storm of disasters—political, economic, even natural—struck Venezuela, among them several of major import for Torre David.

A NEW CONSTITUTION

With just two months in office behind him, Chávez proposed a new Venezuelan constitution to replace that which had been in effect since 1961. In record time, the new National Constituent Assembly drafted that document and, following a popular referendum, the new constitution took effect in December 1999.

One provision in particular was especially significant for the eventual occupiers of Torre David and other squatters. Article 82 reads, in part: "Every person has the right to adequate, safe, comfortable, and hygienic housing with essential basic services, including a habitat that humanizes the family, the neighborhood, and community relations." It further stipulates that the realization of this right is "the shared responsibility of citizens and the State in all areas."[43]

---

40 Margarita López Maya, "Hugo Chávez Frías: His Movement and His Presidency," in *Venezuelan Politics in the Chávez Era,* ed. Steve Ellner and Daniel Hellinger, (Boulder: Lynne Rienner Publishers, Inc., 2003), 73–91. The MBR-200 was a clandestine group formed by Chávez and other young military officers in 1982, with the intent of "rescu[ing] the values of the fatherland, dignify[ing] the military career, and fight[ing] against corruption." The MBR-200 began as a discussion group of sorts, but turned to more concrete action after the events of the Caracazo,

in which many young officers grew uncomfortable with their orders to subdue the civilian population.
41 Tarver and Frederick, *The History of Venezuela,* 149.
42 Ibid., 148.
43 Asamblea Nacional Constituyente, Caracas, 1999. "Constitution of the Bolivarian Republic of Venezuela." Caracas: Ministerio de Comunicación e Información, 2006. http://www.analitica.com/bitblioteca/venezuela/constitucion_ingles.pdf.

In the years since his first election, Chávez has increasingly given priority to the notion of rural land allocation for universal housing. In speeches and television broadcasts, he routinely makes reference to *latifundios,* agricultural "estates of at least 5,000 hectares, or about 12,350 acres" that he asserts are "idle" or under-used.[44] Chávez contends that such "idle" land should be expropriated by the government and distributed to the poor, as a way both to satisfy the enormous and growing demand for housing amongst the poor and to increase Venezuela's national production of agricultural goods.[45]

Initially, there was no clear legal basis for land expropriation. Relying on passionate rhetoric, however, Chávez left no doubt that—in the interest of the nation and the people—he supported public, if still technically illegal, action: squatting and land appropriation by individuals and groups. He emphasized the precedence of "social property" over "private property" and gradually built up the legal foundation for government land expropriation through a stream of presidential decrees.

Though the land reform program focused initially on large agrarian estates—whether the land was being farmed or rented to oil companies for drilling—it wasn't long before the language of the presidential decrees began to include, implicitly at first, the barrios appropriated and occupied by the poor, as well as significant abandoned urban properties. But private rural and urban properties were equally at the mercy of inconsistent and often vague policies, subject to ad hoc interpretation. In such an environment, ownership of assets and land is always in doubt, thus all but wiping out the exchange value of property. By simultaneously encouraging the poor to seize "idle" property and attempting to maintain a government founded on the rule of law, the administration has generated a hostile environment of contradiction, confusion, and coercion.[46]

Having used his command of rhetoric to encourage expropriation, Chávez turned to quasi-legal measures. Among the first was the *Ley de Tierras,* established by presidential decree in November 2001, which paved the way for government redistribution of public land to peasants.[47] Soon thereafter, in February 2002, Chávez issued another decree turning over housing titles to those already occupying government-owned land, as well as to those who had been in occupation of any land for more than ten years.[48]

The codification of squatters' rights was cemented with additional presidential decrees, including No. 1,666, which granted to Venezuelans living in self-built homes on occupied land—in the barrios overlooking Caracas, for instance—the right "to appeal to the government for title to the land."[49] This

44 Juan Forero, "Venezuela Land Reform Looks to Seize Idle Farmland," *New York Times,* January 30, 2005, http://query.nytimes.com/gst/fullpage.html?res=9400EF DD153BF933A05752C0A9639C8B63&pagewanted=all.
45 Many property-owners whose land was seized have never been compensated.
46 The contradiction is evident, for instance, in the use of "citizens" and "residents" alternately as synonyms and antonyms. And, as Zachary Lown notes in his article, "The Conflict Between State-led Revolution and Popular Militancy in Venezuela," "Inherent within the Bolivarian Revolution is the conflict between working class activism and the rule of law in a constitutional democracy."
47 Forero, "Venezuela Land Reform Looks to Seize Idle Farmland."
48 Tamara Pearson, "New Venezuelan Law Turns Unused Urban Land Into Public Land," *venezuelanalysis.com.* August 16, 2009, http://venezuelanalysis.com/news/4726.
49 Gregory Wilpert, "Venezuela's Quiet Housing Revolution: Urban Land Reform," *venezuelanalysis.com,* September 12, 2005, http://venezuelanalysis.com/analysis/1355.

prompted the formation of thousands of Urban Land Committees (CTUs)—co-operative organizations composed of families occupying contiguous land—which advocated for land titles.

Between 2002 and 2010, additional laws and decrees gave the state increasing control over decisions regarding land distribution. Most were officially justified as serving the interests of housing and agricultural development, and they were accompanied by promises to build vast numbers of houses for the poor.[50] While the language of these directives was often vague and confusing, the Urban Land Law, passed by unanimous vote of the National Assembly in August 2009, could not have been clearer or more explicit: it provided that "unused urban land is at the service of the public."[51]

NATURE TAKES SIDES

In December 2010, Caracas was inundated with devastating floods—a common occurrence—that threatened the stability of hillside barrios and the safety of their residents. Estimates put the deaths at 25; 5,000 *caraqueños* were displaced from their homes.[52] The disaster should have surprised no one: in 2001, a multidisciplinary commission from Columbia University undertook a risk assessment and developed a map showing that, at a minimum, 20 percent of the existing barrios were in high-risk areas.[53]

In response to the crisis, Chávez offered up space for the homeless in Miraflores, the presidential palace, as well as in government buildings and in some private hotels.[54]

The Venezuelan parliament, too, acted swiftly, passing an enabling law that same month that granted Chávez 18 months to pass laws by presidential decree.[55] Was this new law a benefit to the displaced, allowing Chávez to act with unhindered speed and efficiency in response to the housing crisis? The government said yes. But critics suggest that the extent of the powers granted to the president was extreme and that Chávez took advantage of a humanitarian crisis to wrest further control from property owners.

Either way, Chávez was on a roll. In February 2011, the Venezuelan Executive Office published the Organic Emergency Law for Lands and Housing, which enables the government to "seize idle urban lands, non-residential

50 See Gran Misión Vivienda Venezuela, http://www.mvh.gob.ve/.

51 Pearson, "New Venezuelan Law Turns Unused Urban Land Into Public Land."

52 Associated Press, "Venezuelan Flood Victims Can Stay at Presidential Palace, Says Hugo Chávez," *The Guardian*, December 2, 2010, http://www.guardian.co.uk/world/2010/dec/02/venezuela-flood-victims-hugo-chavez.

53 At the time, Brillembourg and Klumpner were on the faculty of Columbia University's Graduate School of Architecture, Planning and Preservation, and Urban-Think Tank was a participant in the commission, developing strategies and plans to address the damage and mitigate future risk; their recommendations were shelved by the government.

54 Chris Kraul, "Venezuela Polarized Over Chavez's Land Policy," *Los Angeles Times*, April 7, 2011, http://articles.

latimes.com/print/2011/apr/07/world/la-fg-venezuela-squatters-20110408.

55 "Venezuela Parliament Gives Hugo Chavez More Powers," *BBC*, December 18, 2010. http://www.bbc.co.uk/news/world-latin-america-12024935.

56 Mayela Armas H., "Emergency Law Paves the Way for Seizure of Lands and Storehouses," trans. Gerardo Cárdenas, *El Universal* (Caracas), February 1, 2011. http://www.eluniversal.com/2011/02/01/en_eco_esp_emergency-law-paves_01A5089293.shtml.

57 Ibid.

58 Felipe González and Carlos Crespo, "TSJ argumentó que invasiones ya no son delito en Venezuela," *El Tiempo*, December 12, 2011, http://eltiempo.com.ve/venezuela/tribunales/tsj-argumento-que-invasiones-ya-no-son-delito-en-venezuela/39480.

buildings and assets required for building housing developments," as well as to "implement urban rearrangement and develop housing projects" on this seized land.[56] The law also granted the Executive Office power over "any essential assets that the government may deem necessary for construction of housing projects," essentially declaring these assets to be "of public utility"; and includes an article stating that "the plots of land can be subject to urgent or temporary occupation" prior to government takeover.[57] This last provision is, of course, of particular relevance to squatter occupations, such as the barrios and Torre David.

The culmination of these decrees is a recent Supreme Court ruling on December 12, 2011, in which it was decided that penalties would not be applied against individuals who occupied agricultural land.[58] In the ruling, the court cited the stipulations of the *Ley de Tierras,* explaining that the ruling corresponded with this law. Supporters of private property fear that this has set an extremely dangerous precedent, and worry that in future cases the ruling could be used against those who seek return of or compensation for land that has been seized.

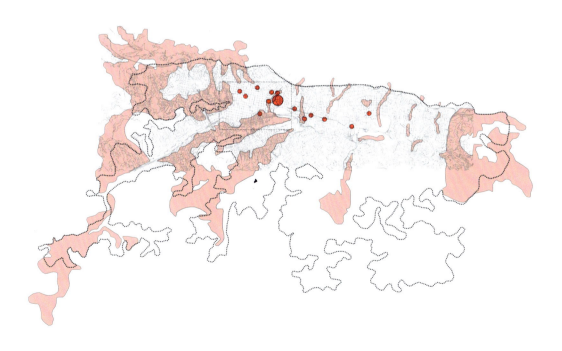

● Torre David
● Invaded Buildings
▨ Informal Settlements (2005)

0   1000   5000

THE PRICE OF REFORM

As of April 2011, an estimated 155 office, apartment, and government buildings in Caracas were occupied by squatters, Torre David among them.[59] Another is one of Torre David's immediate neighbors, Sambil la Candelaria, planned as the latest in a chain of sleek mega-malls. Even as the Sambil mall was under construction, to the delighted anticipation of the neighborhood, it was also under official attack: Chávez referred to it as "a monster of capitalism."[60] It is no surprise, then, that, following the torrential rains in December 2010, the government expropriated the Sambil mall, which had been on the verge of opening for business. Inside the parking garage, the authorities established a 3,000-person homeless shelter.[61]

Local residents are deeply upset by the presence of the shelter; they cite the clothes hanging out to dry and rubbish tossed from the building as both eyesores and hazards for passersby.[62] One article, published in *El Universal* in September 2011, implies that the Sambil building is another Torre David[63]— in other words, just another slum.

In the overall context of contemporary Venezuela, including the country's unstable property rights and values, Torre David would appear to be without any particular distinction.[64] But appearances can be deceiving, and Torre David is, indeed, *sui generis,* both for the degree of organization and cohesion among its residents and for the sheer scale of the occupied structure.

59 Kraul, "Venezuela Polarized Over Chavez's Land Policy."

60 "Chávez retoma paralización del Sambil La Candelaria," *El Universal* (Caracas), June 11, 2009, http://www.eluniversal.com/2009/06/11/ccs_ava_chavez-retoma-parali_11A2383971.shtml.

61 Rafael Rodríguez, "Sambil La Candelaria pasará a ser refugio para damnificados," *El Universal* (Caracas), December 2, 2010, http://www.eluniversal.com/2010/12/02/pol_ava_sambil-la-candelaria_02A4807773.shtml.

62 Delia Meneses, "Convivencia se hace tensa en predios de Sambil Candelaria," *El Universal* (Caracas), January 1, 2012, http://www.eluniversal.com/caracas/120112/convivencia-se-hace-tensa-en-predios-de-sambil-candelaria.

63 Delia Meneses, "Un barrio en Sambil Candelaria," *El Universal* (Caracas), September 23, 2011, http://www.eluniversal.com/2011/09/23/un-barrio-en-sambil-candelaria.shtml.

64 For each of ten categories, the Heritage Foundation's Index of Economic Freedom uses a point system in which 100 is the highest and zero the lowest. In the 2012 Index, Venezuela received a 5 in the "Property Rights" category, putting it, with North Korea, at rock bottom. A brief related report notes that, in Venezuela, "the threat of government expropriation remains high." For more information see www.heritage.org/index/country/venezuela.

THE OCCUPATION

On September 17, 2007, a group of *caraqueños* was evicted from a squat in La Candelaria; searching for shelter, they turned their gaze toward Torre David. That same day people in the barrios of Caracas began receiving cell phone calls and text messages from "professional" squatters, urging them to converge on and occupy Torre David. Like a grapevine, the word grew tentacles and spread until that evening when, in a heavy rain, a large number of families appeared at the entrance to the complex.[65] The two guards on duty took one look at the mass of drenched humanity, turned over their arms, and opened the gates. Thus began the current occupation of Torre David, which has become one of the world's largest vertical squats.

Those who entered the complex on the first evening of the invasion and in the days following quickly staked out space in the ground floor lobby, establishing communal kitchens, setting up tents and other makeshift shelters, and delimiting their territory. Many people came from other invasions and barrios in the surrounding area, flooded out by tropical rain and driven by the promise of better housing closer to jobs in the city. Some families, wary of the unknown conditions inside the Tower, sent one representative to investigate before shuttling the entire clan through the city and out of the rain. Word of this gargantuan, empty, open space spread rapidly, and soon friends and family members of the original occupiers gathered. Three days later, their numbers had grown exponentially. There was little privacy, but a great deal of space available to each family, as well as the hope that the authorities might turn a blind eye. During the first few weeks, as the new arrivals waited to see if they'd be evicted, leaving the space amounted to risking forfeiture of one's stake. Family members guarded their space in shifts—a relay-style, endurance occupation.

As the immediate threat of eviction began to subside, the new inhabitants, urged by the original initiators of the invasion to occupy the rest of the tower, began to explore the whole complex, evaluating the potential for habitation of various spaces. Together they cleaned Torre David, floor by floor, removing the rubble and trash that had accumulated since the Tower's abandonment, and allocated spaces for each family. Gradually, they organized the construction of balustrades and painted communal spaces and private apartments. Through group organization and hard work, each floor soon had 15 families. Initially, only Edificio A was occupied. In 2009, Edificio A was estimated to house 200 families. The location was especially advantageous for informal vendors, greatly reducing the distance and time from home to work and providing storage space for their carts.

65 Depending upon the person who owns the narrative,
the exact number of people varies from 200 to 2,000.

Over time, Torre David became more than a squat—it was evolving into a home, a community, a way of life. But it would be a mistake to assume that safety, serenity, and stability had finally become the norm in Caracas, least of all in a barrio.

At 3pm on the afternoon of April 9, 2012, between 100 and 300 officers from an assortment of Venezuelan security forces raided Torre David, searching for Guillermo Cholele, the Costa Rican commercial attaché to Venezuela.[66] Cholele was kidnapped in Caracas the previous evening; shortly thereafter, his family received a phone call from the kidnappers, demanding ransom. Officers with the Extortion and Kidnapping Division of the Scientific, Criminal and Forensic Investigation Agency (CICPC) traced the phone signal to Torre David.

According to reports by *El Universal,* special security forces entered the Tower from the ground floor and by helicopter, barring people from entering or exiting the building as apartments were searched. Not only were the residents upset and frightened at being separated from children and other family members in the confusion of the raid, they were outraged by the security forces' rough treatment. Residents contend that security forces stole valuable electronics (cell phones, computers, televisions, and cameras) and money, and damaged walls, doors, furniture, and appliances.

Early the following morning, Cholele was released by his kidnappers and established contact with the police and his family. Vindicated of their innocence by the release of the diplomat, but no less infuriated by the raid and evacuation, residents of the Tower gathered outside the Ministerio del Interior y de Justicia on April 11 to protest the abuses committed by security forces.[67] Five official representatives from the Tower went to the Office of the Interior to demand explanations for the poor treatment and the theft of personal belongings.[68]

The raid and the residents' ongoing struggle for official recognition and rights make abundantly evident the precariousness of their circumstances. While the residents freely acknowledge that they occupied the Tower without official approval from the landowner (FOGADE), the pattern of legislative initiatives, judicial decisions, and presidential decrees—not to mention Chávez's public declarations—would have emboldened them to believe they had a degree of entitlement. Moreover, the insufficiency and inadequacy of housing in Caracas and the residents' efforts to remedy that for themselves cast an aura of legitimacy over their occupation of Torre David.

The government continues to face a widespread squatting movement in which Torre David serves perhaps as the largest and most prominent example of illegal occupation. According to the March 5, 2012 edition of *El Nacional* newspaper, almost 50 buildings in La Candelaria remain invaded, and many of the capital's squatter settlements are concentrated in the Libertador Municipality.[69]

66 According to an online article from *El Universal* posted on the afternoon of the raid, over 100 security officers descended upon the tower by ground and air ("Police Force Raids Confinanzas"). A second article, posted the next day, puts that number at 350 (Ramírez, "Torre de David sospechosa de secuestro").

67 "Familias de la Torre Confinanzas protestan en el Ministerio del Interior," *El Universal* (Caracas), April 11, 2012, http://playball.eluniversal.com/caracas/120411/familias-de-la-torre-confinanzas-protestan-en-el-ministerio-del-interi.

68 Ibid.

69 Maolis Castro, "Libertador es territorio de invasiones," *El Nacional* (Caracas), March 5, 2012.

For the Venezuelan government to confront and attempt to reverse the extra-legal occupation of Torre David would be to undermine its own explicit ideology and implicit encouragement. Torre David remains a home for more than 3,000 people. To some, the Tower is simply a crude patchwork of improvisation—a blemish on the face of Caracas, ostensibly a source of violence and insecurity. For those who have nowhere else to go, Torre David is a safe haven, a source of pride, and a home. For now.

AREA OF STUDY – 1 KM²
PROGRAM

■ Invaded   4.200 Inhabitants
■ Barrio   857 Inhabitants
‐ ‐ ‐ CA Metro
‐ ‐ ‐ Metrobús

1. Sambil Commercial Center
2. BBVA Provincial Bank
3. Galerías Avila Commercial Center
4. Alexander Von Humboldt (UAH) University
5. Mercantil Bank
6. Dr. J. M. De Los Ríos Children's Hospital
7. C.A. Caracas Electricity (EDC)
8. Red Cross
9. Church of Mary, Help of Christians
10. College And Oratory of San Francisco De Sales
11. Mosque Ibrahim Ibin Abdul Aziz Al-ibrahim
12. St. Charbel Church

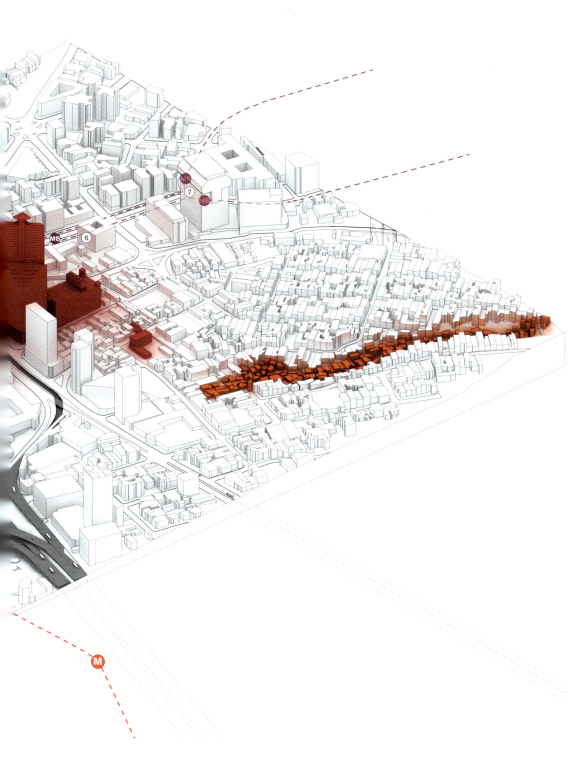

AREA OF STUDY – 1 KM²
PROGRAM

- Invaded — 4.200 Inhabitants
- Barrio — 857 Inhabitants
- Government — 353.8 m²
- Religious — 50.4 m²
- Health — 101.3 m²
- Education — 48.3 m²
- Cultural — 22.3 m²
- Commercial — 252.7 m²
- Bank — 194.000 m²
- Office — 45.4 m²
- Housing — 15.500 Inhabitants
- Parking — 1101.7 m²
- --- CA Metro
- --- Metrobús

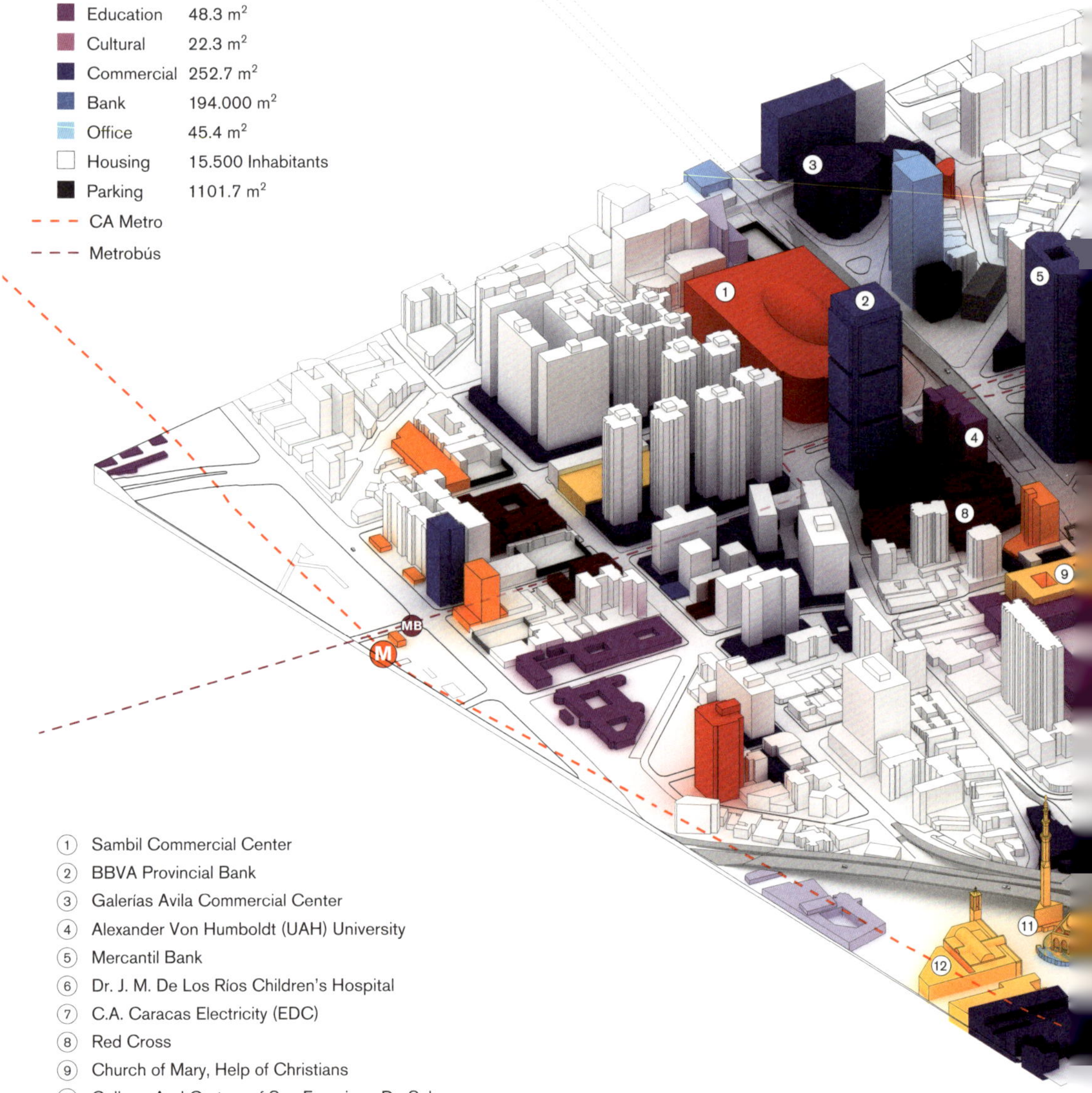

1. Sambil Commercial Center
2. BBVA Provincial Bank
3. Galerías Avila Commercial Center
4. Alexander Von Humboldt (UAH) University
5. Mercantil Bank
6. Dr. J. M. De Los Rios Children's Hospital
7. C.A. Caracas Electricity (EDC)
8. Red Cross
9. Church of Mary, Help of Christians
10. College And Oratory of San Francisco De Sales
11. Mosque Ibrahim Ibin Abdul Aziz Al-ibrahim
12. St. Charbel Church

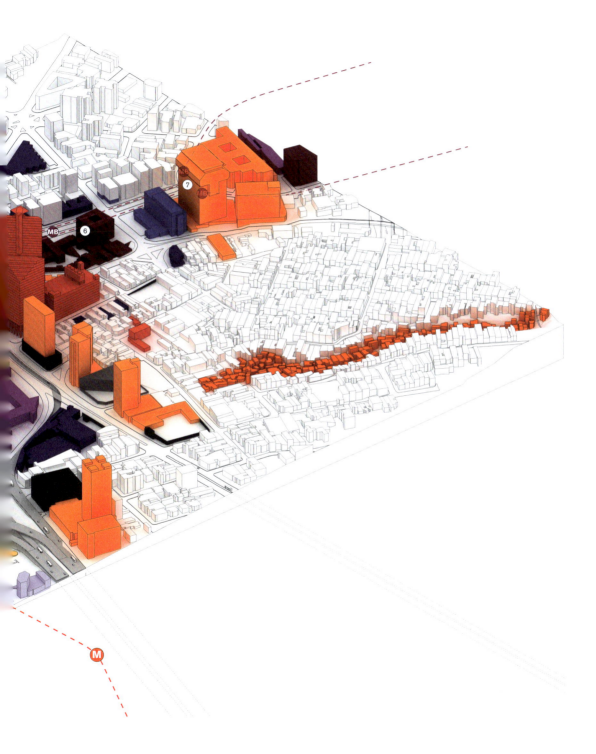

Many *caraqueños'* perceptions of Torre David are
based solely on their view of its exterior.

For safety improvements, such as the construction of handrails and barriers, resourceful residents have used many of the site's leftover building materials.

Along Avenida Urdaneta, directly outside the complex's walls, many residents set up small stands to sell food and goods.

"When we first got here, there was no power supply. So we started to talk to people that had the skills— people with an electrician's background. We met at the ground level and opened the access to the underground power supply. We tried to set up the first electrical phase because we needed to live in these spaces; people needed to be comfortable, so they needed electricity. We knew that what we were doing was illegal, but it was beneficial to the new residents— we did it so that they would have a normal lifestyle."

—Jorge Morales, head electrician and resident of Torre David.

II: PRES.

ENT

STARTING OUT

Ordo ab chao[1]

It is impossible to live in Caracas and not know Torre David. It made news when the development was announced. It made news when it was under construction. And it made news again when the financing collapsed and all work ceased. More recently, it has made local and international news for its occupation and "re-purposing." It is also a distinct physical and symbolic presence and an unmistakable and inescapable feature of Caracas' cityscape.

As architects, urban designers, and *caraqueños* ourselves, we established Caracas Think Tank in 1993 as a way to bring together architects and urbanists to consider how we might create a new strategic urban plan for the city.[2] Even as we explored, worked in, and wrote about various barrios, we had Torre David in mind as a laboratory for a different kind of informal settlement. As early as 2003, we contacted FOGADE, which had taken possession of the complex, to find out what their intentions might be and whether we could assist in whatever efforts they might be planning. Unfortunately, the issues surrounding Torre David became highly politicized in the context of Chávez's election, and we were compelled to retreat to the sidelines.

Nevertheless, we kept a watchful eye on Torre David, as, in 2007 the current population moved in and began to modify and adapt the structure to their needs. Finally, in 2008, we decided to try once more to become involved and to learn just how Torre David was being used. This was no simple task: over the course of three years, we made routine—and routinely unsuccessful—efforts to reach the community leaders by any means possible, including frequent visits to the gates of the complex. It wasn't until 2011, with our proposal to help redesign the façade for safety and aesthetics, that we were able to begin our investigations and interventions.[3]

1 "Out of chaos comes order," among the oldest mottos of the Freemasons who—as philosophical builders—use as architectural symbolism the tools of medieval stonemasons to teach moral and ethical lessons.
2 We later changed our name to Urban-Think Tank as we broadened our research base and began working in other cities as well.

3 For these endeavors, we received a research grant from the Schindler Group and support from the ETH Zürich.

An original model of the Centro Financiero
Confinanzas, 1992.

Photo: Inmuebles Magazine/Pineda y Lorenzo

Torre David, 2011.

Even then, for all the time we spent in Torre David and with its residents, we were never unreservedly welcomed, nor could we entirely pierce the barriers of wariness and suspicion they erected against all outsiders. We had the approval and assent of the leadership, but were escorted everywhere, our comings and goings strictly limited and monitored, our activities carefully watched. Occasionally, the residents' guard would drop. We would be invited to share meals, to attend church services and meetings and birthday parties. We even spent the night on spare mattresses when it grew late and residents feared for our safety traveling in such a notoriously dangerous city as Caracas. But just when we thought we had achieved real familiarity and trust, we would return to cold shoulders and skepticism; residents would impede our access to the property, we could not take measurements or gather information. And we would have to begin again to prove our loyalty and absence of a hidden agenda.

This is by no means a criticism of the Torre David community. Given the precariousness of their occupancy—indeed, of their lives—the residents remain understandably alert and guarded against outsiders whose intrusion may rock the delicate stability they have managed to create. They have little reason to believe someone who claims to be an ally; and today's ally may be tomorrow's opponent. We may have arrived with an invitation to help the residents; we may have had a long history of working compatibly and collaboratively with residents of the city's barrios; we may have been highly respectful of this community and its members. Still, we were "them," they were "us."

PERSPECTIVE IS EVERYTHING

Even after a year of intensive interaction, it remains extremely difficult to describe Torre David's physical and organizational structure. The high-rise is an irony, an oxymoron, a contradiction in itself: a success of sorts within a failure; a barrio that is also a gated community; a hierarchical, authoritarian anarchy. Within its walls, individual initiatives and freedoms are in dynamic tension with communal needs and obligations. From the outside, it is either a blight on the neighborhood and emblematic of everything that is wrong and dangerous about Caracas; or it is a potential safe zone, a new and better way of living, however precarious and temporary. Perspective and expectation determine whether one despises or envies Torre David's residents.

Like everyone else, members of U-TT bring our personal and professional histories with us wherever we are; we cannot escape our training and experiences, our assumptions about what "squatter" and "barrio" mean. We make a great effort, on the other hand, to look for, understand, and integrate into our understanding that which does not fit our preconceptions. As we worked with Torre David, we found that many of our expectations did not stand up to the reality.

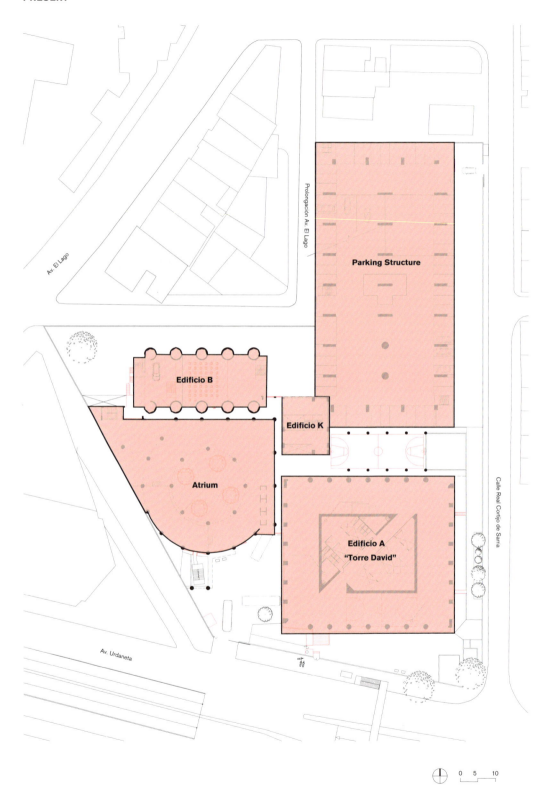

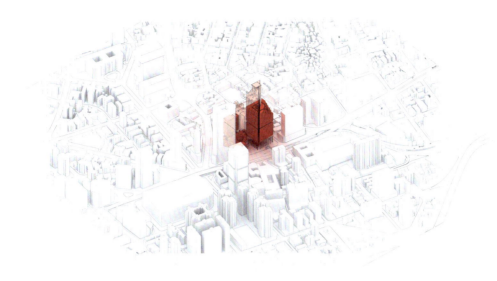

Photo: U-TT/Daniel Schwartz

PHYSICAL ORGANIZATION IN FLUX

As we noted at the beginning of this book, Torre David is not one but a cluster of structures made up of five distinct volumes. The 45-story tower itself—known previously in the developer's plans as Edificio A, but generally referred to here as the high-rise—is the primary site of the occupation, where the majority of residents live and which contains the greatest concentration of social services. Adjacent to the high-rise is Edificio B, a 19-story structure originally intended for executive suites and now housing an Evangelical Pentecostal church and a growing number of new residents. Between these two structures is Edificio K, a 19-story empty shell, which serves to connect the two larger buildings on floors 6–17.

The fourth structure is the 10-story parking garage, which serves not only its intended purpose but also as an informal access ramp to the high-rise. For security reasons, the original design excluded any direct access from the parking structure to the other buildings. The current residents broke through the reinforced concrete walls, creating openings from which small footbridges lead into Edificio K on each floor. The fifth structure is the 30-m-high atrium, where members of the Tower cooperative often gather for meetings and a few residents have built apartments.

At present, there are some 750 families, totaling approximately 3,000 inhabitants, occupying the high-rise up through the 28th floor. Until recently, some families were still living in tents on that floor, a practice the leadership disallowed as of earlier in 2012. Without a working elevator, the community's leadership decided to limit access to the upper floors, for reasons of safety. Nevertheless, even given the physical burden of the long climb, the upper floors are considered desirable by those seeking to move in. From the 29th floor to the rooftop helipad, the building is untouched, looking much as it did in 1994 when construction ceased.

In addition to living quarters, Torre David has dedicated common spaces that serve to bring the residents together in formal and semi-formal ways. Chief among these is the community's Evangelical Pentecostal church, the *Puerta del Cielo Casa de Dios* (Heaven's Door House of God), which residents began constructing in early 2010 on the ground floor of Edificio B. While waiting for the completion of the larger church space, the congregation gathers at least three times a week in a temporary church on the first floor of Edificio B, for services led by Alexander Daza. The families of Torre David are primarily Evangelical Pentecostal Christians, a notable anomaly in a mainly Catholic city, but not so in the squatter population. This particular settlement fits into

Edificio K connects Edificios A, B, and the parking garage.

Residents break through an existing wall to create new pathways for movement.

Photos: U-TT/Daniel Schwartz

Residents on the basketball court.

A man with an injured foot rests on his way up
to his apartment.

a larger Pentecostal squatter movement with complex socio-economic ties to housing shortages and property law.[4]

No less important to the residents than church, evidently, is basketball, which also functions as a common ground. On the ground level, between the parking structure and the high-rise is a large, multi-purpose court, flanked by six columns on each side and defined by brightly painted boundary lines and two nets affixed to walls at opposite ends of the space. A few large painted symbols are scattered across the floor, faded by the scuffing of daily use: a red sun surrounded by yellow flames, a red and blue pinwheel designating center court, a small blue star, and the words *"Lucha por la Juventud"* (Fight for Youth) stretching across the expanse of the court. A carefully painted mural on the wall at one end of the court includes the phrases *"Dios es Vida," "Club Deportivo,"* and *"Cacique de Cultura Venezuela."*

Residents of the tower have a basketball team that plays against teams from the neighborhood and surrounding barrios. The cooperative provides equipment and uniforms for the team, and there is an appointed sports coordinator who organizes and trains the players. The court space itself is well regulated, and it is forbidden to swear on the court or to play without sportswear. The cooperative hopes eventually to build a roof over the exposed space in order to prevent accidents caused by objects falling from the upper floors and to allow for play during inclement weather.

There are less obviously organized areas for informal and serendipitous socialization. On the 28th floor, several residents, led by the brothers Frankenstein and Grabiel and their friend, Deivis, have created a small gym using parts from the inoperative elevators and air-conditioning units to fashion free weights and a bench-press. That same floor has an extended "balcony" facing northwest, where some of the women often bring couches and chairs to socialize while they keep on eye on their young children who—in defiance of the dangerous 28-story drop—run, ride tricycles, and rush about on scooters. The mothers acknowledge the risk, but insist that their children know not to approach the edge of the balcony.

On other floors, too, residents use unoccupied or common spaces where they stop and talk, exchange news, and cement the bonds of proximity. The stairs are, of course, a primary informal meeting place and the physical manifestation of a community grapevine. Since the one accessible stairway in the high-rise is the only means of vertical circulation within that structure, sooner or later everyone passes everyone else.

Despite certain immovable and unalterable features, much of Torre David is in a near-constant state of evolution and modification, physically and socially, spheres that continually influence one another. Early in the occupation,

4 Across Caracas, the Evangelical Pentecostals have taken over former theaters, cinemas, supermarkets, and other large spaces in buildings owned by FOGADE, converting these into churches and social centers. While this group may still appear anomalous in a predominantly Catholic city, it increasingly shares with Mormons and Jehovah's Witnesses, as well as the local cults of Maria-Lionza and Gregorio Hernandez, the reshaping of the religious landscape, especially in the low-income neighborhoods. For further information see Rafael Sánchez, "Seized by the Spirit: The Mystical Foundation of Squatting among Pentecostals in Caracas (Venezuela) Today," *Public Culture* 20, no.2 (Spring 2008): 267–305, doi:10.1215/08992363-2007-026.

Level –02 Level –01 Level 00 Level 01 – Ground Floor Level 02

Level 08 Level 09 Level 10 Level 11 Level 12

Level 18 Level 19 Level 20 Level 21 Level 22

Level 28 Level 29 Level 30 Level 31 Level 32

Level 38 Level 39 Level 40 Level 41 Level 42

Apartment Electrical

Store Water Tank

Sports Public

Administration Parking

Religious Unoccupied

Physical Organization in Flux

Level 03   Level 04   Level 05   Level 06   Level 07

Level 13   Level 14   Level 15   Level 16   Level 17

Level 23   Level 24   Level 25   Level 26   Level 27

Level 33   Level 34   Level 35   Level 36   Level 37

Level 43   Level 44   Level 45   Level 45

0   50   100

for instance, only the ground floor was electrified and many residents still lived in tents. Almost all spaces and services—cooking and toilet facilities, among others—were shared. As an informal communal organization began to emerge, spaces were systematically divided and allocated to each family; people began to make the adaptations necessary to give individuals their own facilities. Over time, this distribution of space eroded the strictly collective organization, giving rise simultaneously to greater individuality with respect to one's own habitation and a stronger framework of overall authority and group responsibilities. The purely ad hoc and informal solutions to spatial, social, sanitary, and technical issues have given way to the more conventional. Indeed, the residents are emphatically not looking to the hillside barrios for inspiration; they are aspirational, taking middle-class apartments as their models. Gladys Flores points to the nearby Parque Central complex as what she hopes will be the future of Torre David.

THE COMMON GROUND
OF COMMUNITY ORGANIZATION

In much the same way, the socio-political organization within Torre David has evolved. Outsiders for the most part remain unaware that the first occupation—a smaller invasion of "undesirables" in 2003 who were eventually evicted by the police—has been replaced by a genuine community, operating as a cooperative and structured with rules, procedures, and a bureaucracy that would not be foreign to anyone living in an upscale cooperative apartment building in cities like New York, Paris, and London.

However informal as its workings may at first appear, the *Asociacion Cooperativa de Vivienda "Casiques de Venezuela," R.L.* was formally registered with and certified by the Autonomous Service of Registries and Notaries (*Servicio Autónomo de Registros y Notarías*) in 2009, with an objective, or mission statement:

> *"[P]romover la construcción de un urbanismo compuesto por viviendas dignas, constituido por apartamentos, casa vecinal, colegio preescolar, maternal, áreas para puestos de estacionamiento y sala de usos multiples."* [5]

The organization, invasion, and settlement of Torre David, as well as the development of social structures and implementation of infrastructural improvements, have all emerged from the community, working in concert. Residents have an uncommon cohesiveness and solidarity with one another, understanding only too well their interdependency for the maintenance of stability and order. This cohesion creates a fortunate common ground on which Torre David's rules and regulations have been built.

Not just anyone can take up residence in Torre David. In the early days of the occupation, prospective residents were permitted to apply for space every Monday between 5pm and 8pm. If they were accepted for residence, they were required to live in tents while waiting for the privilege of securing a formal, dedicated space they could develop. Now that the Tower's affairs are more organized and regulated, most of the spaces have been filled by families, and no new residents are admitted until there is a vacancy. As with conventional cooperative residences, no family owns their space. If the occupants receive more than three citations for infractions of the general code of conduct—holding large and noisy parties too often, littering, instances of domestic violence, and the like—they are asked to leave, a three-strikes rule that remains in force. On

5 Nancy Velasco, "Se consolida invasión de la Torre de David," *El Universal* (Caracas), April 17, 2010. Author's translation: "[T]o promote the construction of an urban environment comprised of dignified housing, composed of apartments, a communal house, a preschool, a kindergarten, areas for parking spaces and a multi-purpose room."

a public notice board in the lobby of Torre David, through which everyone who uses the pedestrian entrance walks, there are frequent updates announcing vacancies, new rules and regulations, and upcoming events.

In addition to a monthly fee of $15 paid by each family to the Cooperative for water, electricity, cleaning of the public spaces, and security, families pay for and own the investments they make in their respective apartments. Some spend virtually nothing on what might be considered capital improvements to the space itself, others as much as $10,000. When a family leaves, incoming tenants often buy the modifications that have been made to the property. In addition, many invest in furniture, a toilet, a stove, and other amenities; these, too, are sold to the newcomers. As we have noted before, the instability of the Venezuelan economy and currency has led most to invest their money in tangibles.

Photo: U-TT/Daniel Schwartz

INVASION

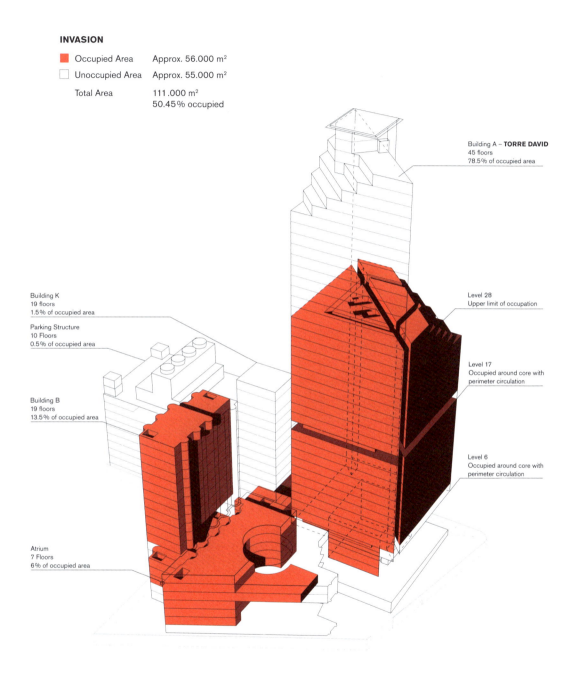

■ Occupied Area	Approx. 56.000 m²	
□ Unoccupied Area	Approx. 55.000 m²	
Total Area	111.000 m² 50.45% occupied	

Building A – **TORRE DAVID**
45 floors
78.5% of occupied area

Level 28
Upper limit of occupation

Level 17
Occupied around core with
perimeter circulation

Level 6
Occupied around core with
perimeter circulation

Building K
19 floors
1.5% of occupied area

Parking Structure
10 Floors
0.5% of occupied area

Building B
19 floors
13.5% of occupied area

Atrium
7 Floors
6% of occupied area

AN AUTOCRATIC DEMOCRACY

Notwithstanding the communal nature of decision-making, it would be a mistake to understand Torre David as a pure representative democracy or as entirely consensus-driven. Its leadership structure is a sequence of concentric circles of influence and authority. The innermost circle, known as "la Directiva" or the Directive, revolves about the president of the cooperative, Alexander "el Niño" Daza, the pastor for the church in Edifico B, and consists of several of Daza's closest associates. Together, they make the ultimate decisions regarding many of the day-to-day operating policies in Torre David and plan for future security and growth. In the second circle are those whose ostensible role is solely to act as intermediaries between the Directive and the residents and as coordinators of such functions as water distribution, the electrical system, and facility cleaning.

Some, however, have considerably more authority. Gladys Flores, who, as the secretary of the cooperative occupies the second circle, actually wields real influence with the Directive, a function of her intelligence, organizational skills, and direct involvement in most operations and planning meetings. Gladys oversees the third circle of leadership, the floor coordinators, who are charged with organizing the space and ensuring that the building systems on his or her respective floor are maintained. Gladys organizes the coordinators' reports, complaints, and requests into manageable memos for consideration by the Directive; she participates in public space planning, filing official paperwork, and management of relations between the cooperative and the municipal government. Gladys has lived on the 15th floor with two of her daughters since 2007; a third daughter also lives on the 15th floor with her husband and their baby. Gladys is both popular and highly respected, making her an effective mediator in disputes between residents. Her knowledge of the workings of the cooperative was invaluable to U-TT, as she helped clarify the hierarchy, describing a mix of bottom-up democratic discussion and consensus that influence the authoritarian decision-making apparatus at the top. Daza has the absolute and final say on everything—but he can be receptive to the suggestions of those below him.

Residents work together during a scheduled community cleanup.

Photo: U-TT/Daniel Schwartz

Gladys Flores (in pink, standing) leads a community meeting
in the atrium.

Photo: U-TT/Markus Kneer

The white gate is the complex's main pedestrian
entrance. Sitting on the bench, chatting with
other residents, is the one of the pastors from the
150   Tower's church.

Security guards work in shifts to ensure the
safety of those living in the Tower.

Community bulletin boards display announce-
ments and photos. Here, a resident has
posted photos of some recent efforts to renovate
the complex.

The ground floor serves as an open public space
for the inhabitants.

From painting the concrete columns and walls to adding
a touch of greenery by planting young palm trees,
residents have worked together to make public spaces
such as the atrium comfortable and welcoming.

MOVING INTO, MOVING AROUND

There are four official ways to enter the Tower complex, one of which, located on Avenida Urdaneta to the south, is devoted exclusively to pedestrian access. Each household is given a magnetic key fob with which to open the door to enter or exit the property. A vehicular entrance, also on Avenida Urdaneta, is used by buses that park in an underground lot under the atrium. Although this entrance formerly served for pedestrians as well—the residents having cut a doorway into the sliding gate—in 2011 they decided to more explicitly differentiate between vehicular and pedestrian access and opened up the previously unused pedestrian door. In March 2012, they build a tall concrete wall to create a barrier between the two entrances and installed a raised security pavilion to monitor both. On the west side of the complex is the entrance to the 10-story parking structure, which is secured with two sliding iron doors. Access via the fourth entrance, on the north side of the complex, is extremely restricted.

Security guards are stationed at the three actively used entrances, rotating in 24-hour shifts. Caracas is a violent and unpredictable city, and security is a top priority for citizens of all socioeconomic levels. Residents of Torre David are no exception. In addition to the security pavilion at the pedestrian entrance, the bus access has a similar shelter for the guards, while the entrance to the parking structure has only a desk and some chairs. Guards are paid a salary for their work above the minimum wage in Venezuela and are equipped with radios to maintain contact with one another, as well as with members of the electricity and water crew and other community leaders. Like doormen in an exclusive apartment building, guards are familiar with all of Torre David's residents and keep careful track of those entering and exiting the complex.

For those residents with cars or motorbikes, or who hire a mototaxi, the ramp of the parking structure now serves as an informal "elevator" for the complex. Mototaxi drivers line up outside the Tower's entrances, or at the top of the garage, and charge small fees (no more than Bs. 20) to ferry people, goods, and building materials up to the 10th floor or down to the street level.

To move horizontally among the structures, the residents have broken holes through the reinforced concrete walls of each of the parking garage's floors and built small footbridges into Edificio K. From there, they access the other two structures. But since the floor slabs, jutting out from Edificio K, do not make contact with those of either Edificio B or the high-rise, there are gaps of 30 cm, and the residents—particularly children—risk a considerable fall when they traverse.

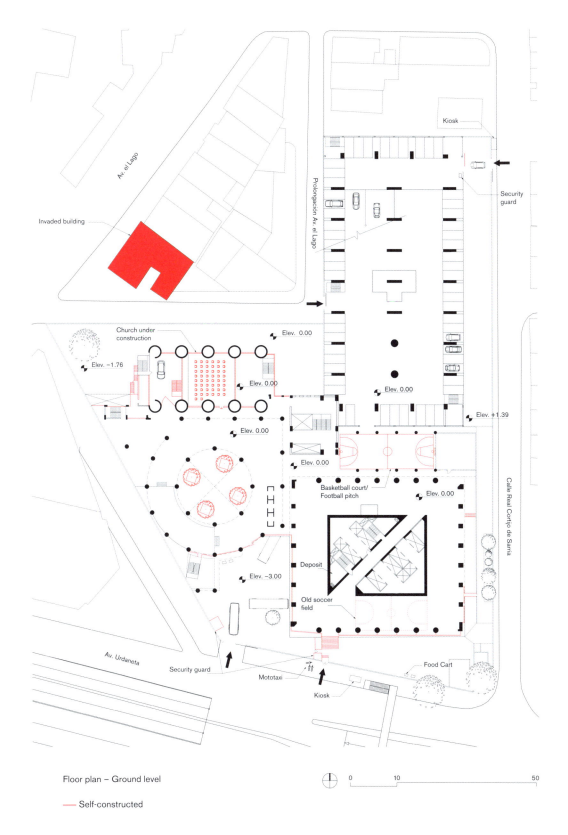

Av. el Lago

Invaded building

Prolongación Av. el Lago

Kiosk

Security
guard

Church under
construction

Elev. 0.00

Elev. −1.76

Elev. 0.00

Elev. 0.00

Elev. 0.00

Elev. +1.39

Elev. 0.00

Elev. 0.00

Basketball court/
Football pitch

Elev. 0.00

Deposit

Old soccer
field

Elev. −3.00

Calle Real Cortijo de Sarria

Av. Urdaneta

Security guard

Mototaxi

Kiosk

Food Cart

Floor plan – Ground level

—— Self-constructed

0   10   50

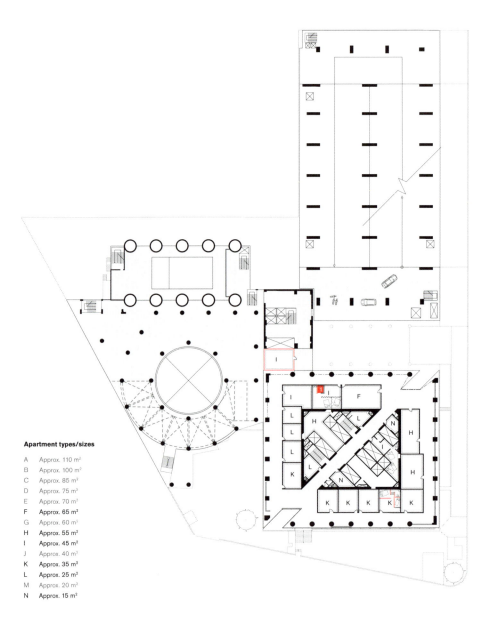

Apartment types/sizes

A   Approx. 110 m²
B   Approx. 100 m²
C   Approx. 85 m²
D   Approx. 75 m²
E   Approx. 70 m²
F   **Approx. 65 m²**
G   Approx. 60 m²
H   **Approx. 55 m²**
I   **Approx. 45 m²**
J   Approx. 40 m²
K   **Approx. 35 m²**
L   **Approx. 25 m²**
M   Approx. 20 m²
N   **Approx. 15 m²**

1 Shop
2 Sewing workshop
3 Gym area
   Public area
—   Self-constructed

Floor plan – Level 6

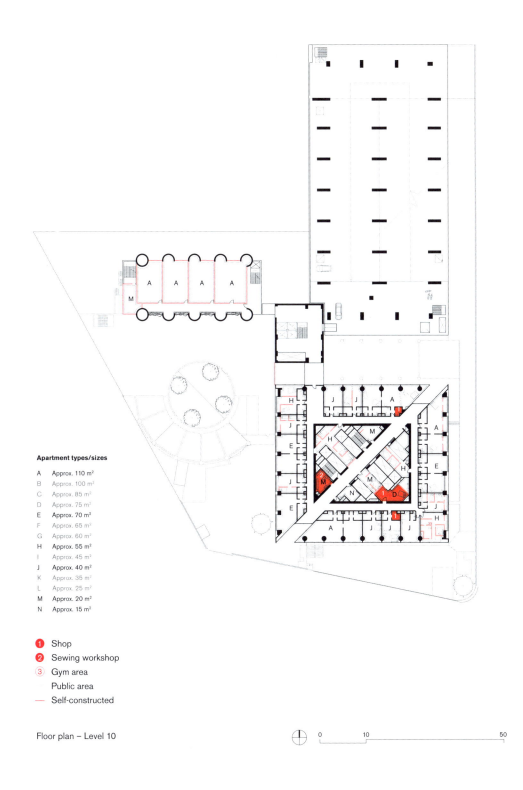

Apartment types/sizes

A   Approx. 110 m²
B   Approx. 100 m²
C   Approx. 85 m²
D   Approx. 75 m²
E   Approx. 70 m²
F   Approx. 65 m²
G   Approx. 60 m²
H   Approx. 55 m²
I   Approx. 45 m³
J   Approx. 40 m²
K   Approx. 35 m²
L   Approx. 25 m²
M   Approx. 20 m²
N   Approx. 15 m²

① Shop
② Sewing workshop
③ Gym area
   Public area
— Self-constructed

Floor plan – Level 10

0   10   50

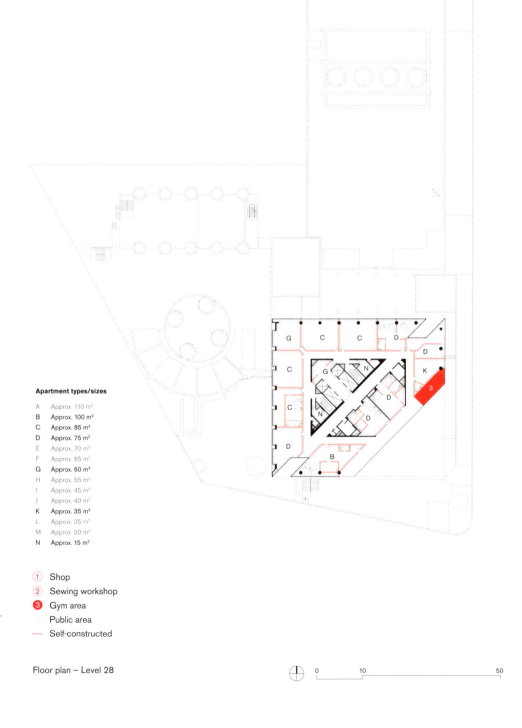

Apartment types/sizes

A   Approx. 110 m²
B   Approx. 100 m²
C   Approx. 85 m²
D   Approx. 75 m²
E   Approx. 70 m²
F   Approx. 65 m²
G   Approx. 60 m²
H   Approx. 55 m²
I   Approx. 45 m²
J   Approx. 40 m²
K   Approx. 35 m²
L   Approx. 25 m²
M Approx. 20 m²
N   Approx. 15 m²

① Shop
② Sewing workshop
❸ Gym area
    Public area
— Self-constructed

Floor plan – Level 28

0   10   50

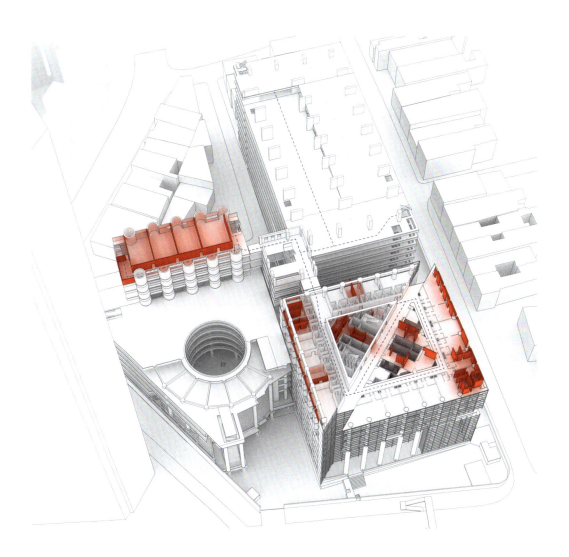

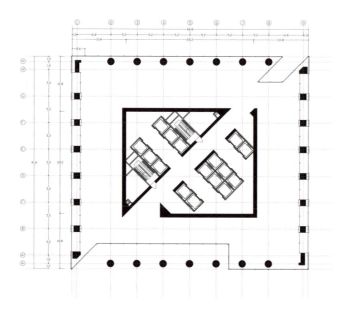

Ground level, pre-occupation.

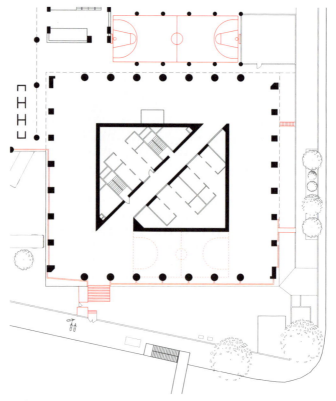

Ground level, post-occupation.

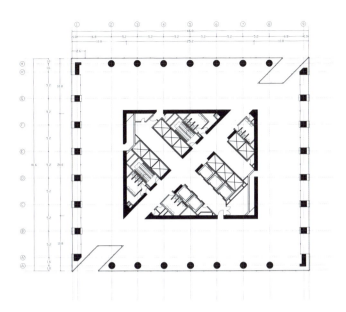

Level 6, pre-occupation.

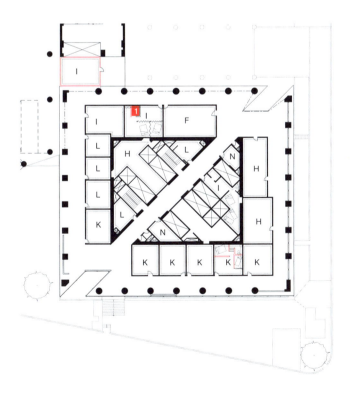

Level 6, post-occupation.

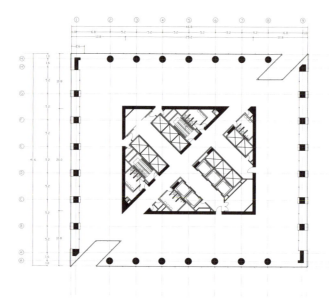

Level 10, pre-occupation.

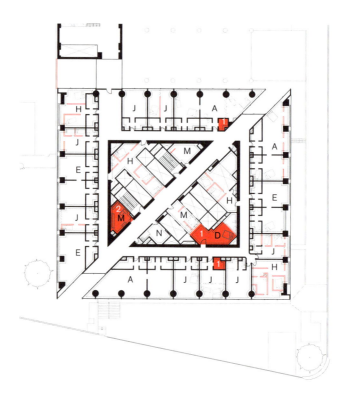

Level 10, post-occupation.

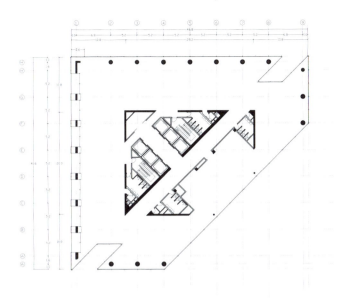

Level 28, pre-occupation.

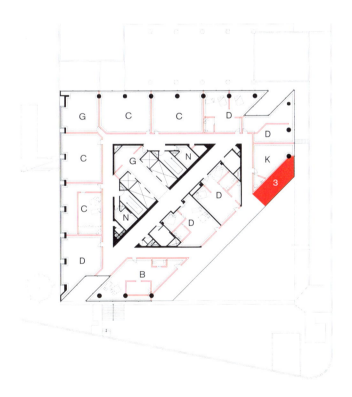

Level 28, post-occupation.

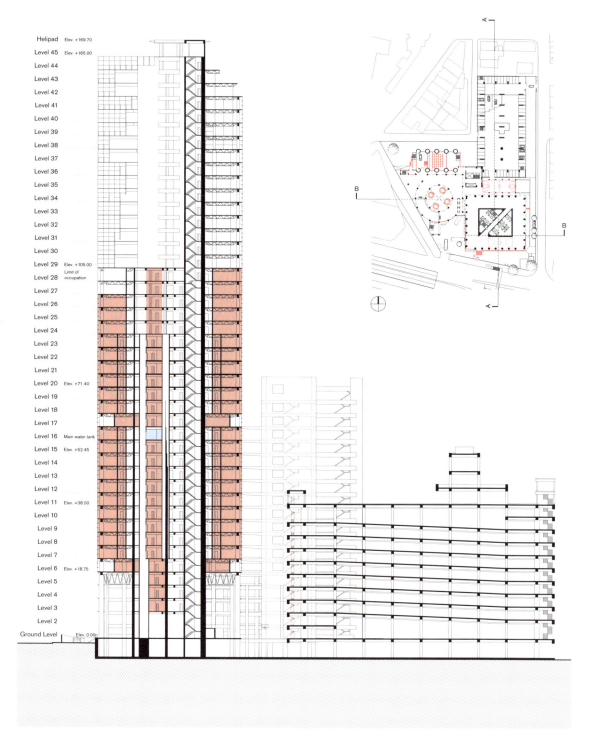

Helipad   Elev. +169.70
Level 45   Elev. +165.00
Level 44
Level 43
Level 42
Level 41
Level 40
Level 39
Level 38
Level 37
Level 36
Level 35
Level 34
Level 33
Level 32
Level 31
Level 30
Level 29   Elev. +105.00
Level 28   Limit of occupation
Level 27
Level 26
Level 25
Level 24
Level 23
Level 22
Level 21
Level 20   Elev. +71.40
Level 19
Level 18
Level 17
Level 16   Main water tank
Level 15   Elev. +52.45
Level 14
Level 13
Level 12
Level 11   Elev. +38.00
Level 10
Level 9
Level 8
Level 7
Level 6   Elev. +18.75
Level 5
Level 4
Level 3
Level 2
Ground Level   Elev. 0.00

Section A-A

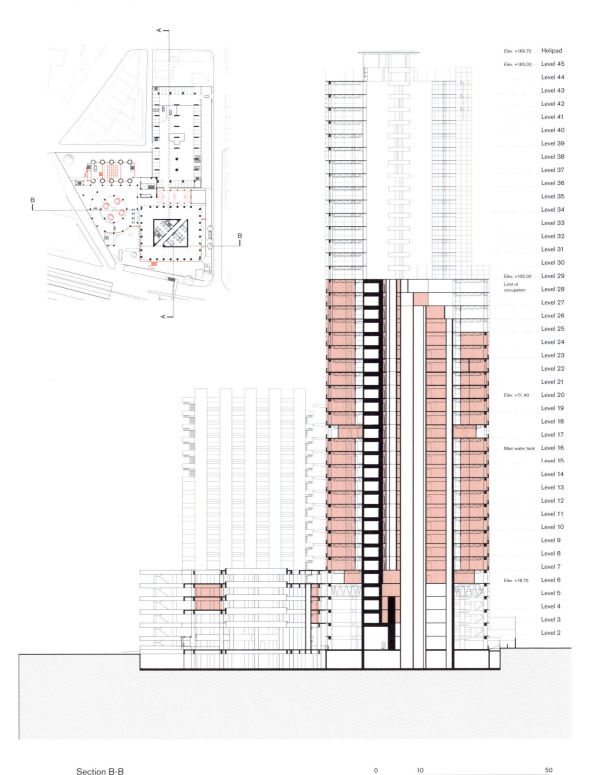

Elev. +169.70	Helipad
Elev. +165.00	Level 45
	Level 44
	Level 43
	Level 42
	Level 41
	Level 40
	Level 39
	Level 38
	Level 37
	Level 36
	Level 35
	Level 34
	Level 33
	Level 32
	Level 31
	Level 30
Elev. +105.00	Level 29
Limit of occupation	Level 28
	Level 27
	Level 26
	Level 25
	Level 24
	Level 23
	Level 22
	Level 21
Elev. +71.40	Level 20
	Level 19
	Level 18
	Level 17
Main water tank	Level 16
	Level 15
	Level 14
	Level 13
	Level 12
	Level 11
	Level 10
	Level 9
	Level 8
	Level 7
Elev. +18.75	Level 6
	Level 5
	Level 4
	Level 3
	Level 2

Section B-B

0   10   50

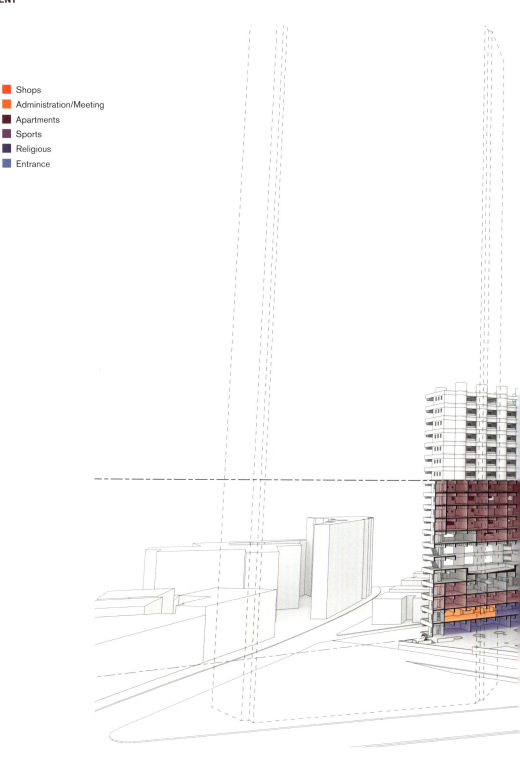

- Shops
- Administration/Meeting
- Apartments
- Sports
- Religious
- Entrance

Stairs are the only means of vertical circulation; the elevator parts were scavenged and sold in the years after the Tower was abandoned. The high-rise has two stairwells, one for use by the residents, the other kept locked, is reserved for infrastructure and can only be opened by a member of the leadership.

Many floors remain partially open to the outside, with no dividing walls; glass panels of the façade have been removed to increase air circulation, leaving gaping holes to the outside. And while some residents have implemented their own safety measures by erecting short brick balcony walls, the possibility of a fatal fall calls for constant vigilance. This ubiquitous danger is compounded by unexpected holes in the floors, encountered throughout the building. The stairs lack handrails, although residents are in the process of constructing their own. Elevator shafts remain open in many instances. Living with these spatial deficiencies, residents must remain alert when moving throughout the complex.

An open elevator shaft.

A gaping hole in the floor.

Floor slabs connecting Edificio B (left) and
Edificio K (right).

Photos: U-TT/Daniel Schwartz

CIRCULATION DIAGRAM

- Tower floor circulation
- Stairs
- Vehicle access
- Pedestrian access

1. External mototaxi path to parking
2. Internal mototaxi path to parking
3. Bus access to underground parking

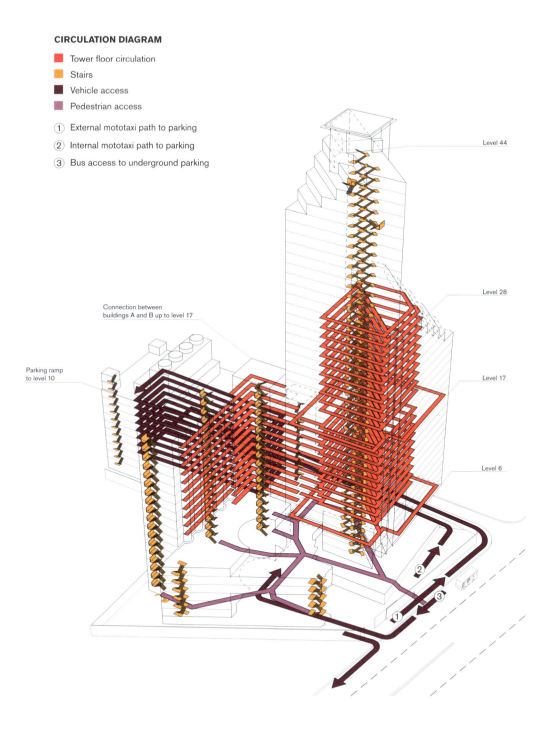

Connection between
buildings A and B up to level 17

Parking ramp
to level 10

Level 44

Level 28

Level 17

Level 6

Almost all residents use the stairwells on a daily
basis, making them central spaces for social
interaction.

In the absence of elevators, hired mototaxis and cars offer rides up the 10 floors of the parking garage, providing residents with quick, easy access to Edificios A and B.

Some residents have set up a small auto
workshop in the parking garage.

The basketball court on the ground floor
is a popular hangout for the Tower's young
residents.

MODIFICATIONS & MATERIALS

To describe the squatters' alterations to Torre David as a slumification or *ranchosis*[6] is both accurate and misleading. Residents look backward, to their experiences of the barrios, in order to move forward, toward a normalized ideal drawn from middle-class standards. Throughout the building, one sees a certain consistency in the use of materials and application of methods in the common spaces and, to an extent, in each family's living area. But there is also considerable eclecticism, born of individual ability, impulse toward experimentation, taste, and financial resources. In general, the adaptive reuse of the building appears to be evolving toward the "normal," or formal, by means of a trial-and-error informality. Thus construction in Torre David combines collective knowledge of the self-built, incremental housing of the barrios with new techniques and strategies that adapt this knowledge to the conditions of the Tower.

For reasons of economy and custom, the most common choice of building material in Torre David is red clay brick, used to construct houses in the barrios. This gives the structures created by the residents the color, texture, and morphologies seen in the barrios. Red bricks are also used to demarcate private space in Torre David, much as they are used in the barrios as a means of claiming territory. Interestingly, one of the *caraqueños* who moved into Torre David at the beginning of the current occupation was a brickmaker, who set up a small shop where he took up his vocation. While other small entrepreneurial efforts scattered through the building have succeeded, his, unfortunately did not. It proved more costly for residents to purchase his bricks than to buy them from the suppliers they had used in the barrios.

Some creative adaptations and design interventions, initially experimental, have proven successful. Breaking through walls that initially separated

6 "Ranchosis" signifies a city dweller's habit of mentally carrying the slum in one's head and reproducing it in one's environment. For further information, see José Tomas Sanabria, "ranchosis," *El Nacional* (Caracas), February 21, 2000, http://www.tomasjosesanabria.com/index.php?mod=paginas&id=13.

the buildings in the complexhas greatly improved circulation; the passage-ways connecting Edificio K with the high-rise have been partially sealed with offset brick walls on each floor, providing a modicum of privacy without losing crucial ventilation. Some floors have painted these walls, using color to give each "neighborhood" a local identity.

Other interventions address a common issue using different methods and materials. To improve security along stairs, hallways, and balconies, residents have employed rebar, scavenged trusses, PVC pipes, and unmortared bricks, to varying degrees of stability and durability. Recycling is both standard and, often, inventive.

An apartment under construction in the atrium.

All photos: U-TT/Daniel Schwartz

INDIVIDUAL INITIATIVE

THE ENTREPRENEURIAL IMPERATIVE

Torre David could rightly be called a mixed-use building, more accurately so, perhaps, than developments planned and programmed for that purpose: the latter strictly quarantine one use from another, usually in horizontal blocks, whereas Torre David's residents have blended uses in an ad hoc fashion. A number of small grocery stores, on different floors of the high-rise, sell essentials, sparing residents the long trip to street level and local shops. The cooperative controls prices in stores from the ground to the 10th floor; merchants must sell their goods at prices regulated by the government. Above the 10th floor, on the other hand, shop owners are permitted to set their prices at one or two *bolívares* more than the government mandate, taking into account the costs and difficulty of transportation. Residents of higher floors are essentially a captive customer base.

Other residents are equally entrepreneurial. A hairdresser, employed by day in one of the city's premier salons, earns additional income by giving residents cheap haircuts in a closet he has rented in Torre David. A window

One of Torre David's successful grocery stores.

Photo: U-TT/Daniel Schwartz

BUILDING PROGRAM

■ Shops
　① Large grocery stores
■ Administration
　② Coordinators' assembly space
■ Sports
　③ Gym terrace
■ Textile workshop
■ Religious
■ Entrance area
　④ Identity check
■ Main trash dump

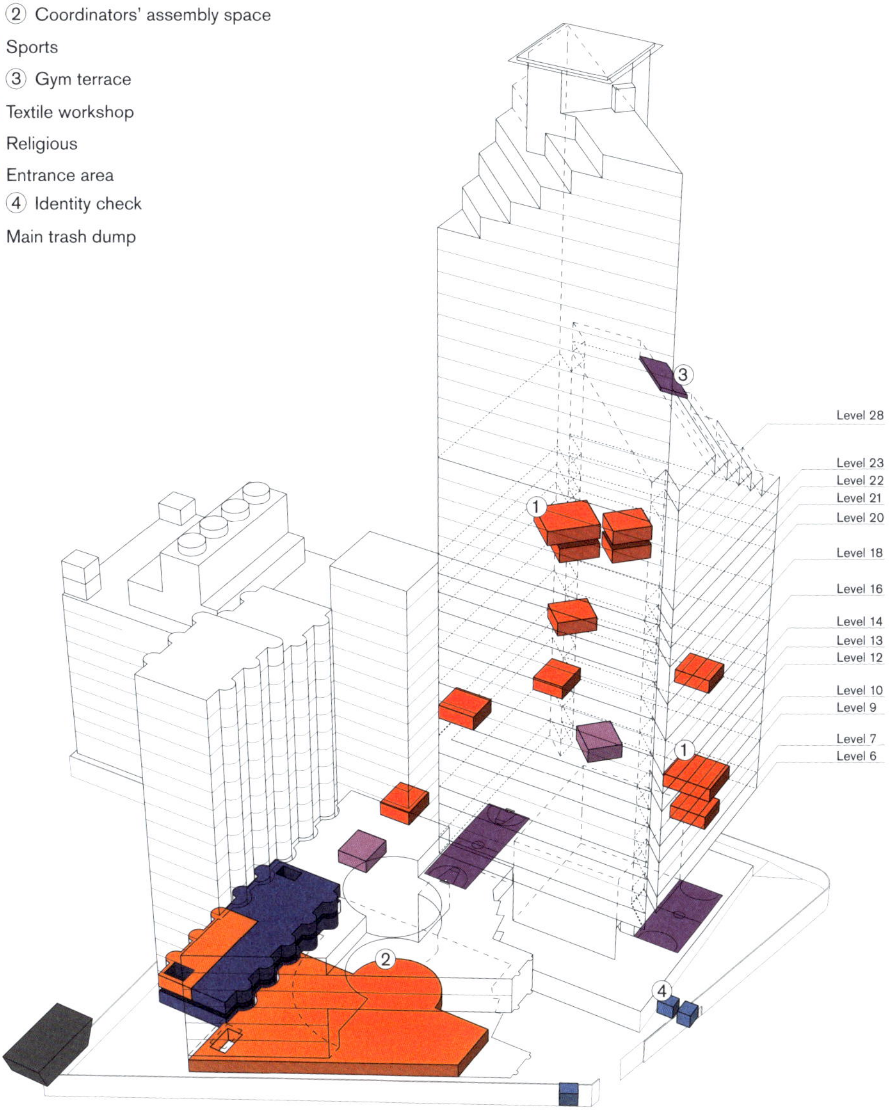

Level 28

Level 23
Level 22
Level 21
Level 20

Level 18

Level 16

Level 14
Level 13
Level 12

Level 10
Level 9

Level 7
Level 6

salvaged from the building serves as his mirror. Another resident runs a tailoring shop from her living room, outfitted with two sewing machines. Still another—a student at the law school of the Bolivarian University of Venezuela—tends a small shop selling office and school supplies in the family apartment. There is also a small snack shop, run out of an alcove next to the front door of the apartment and separated from the hallway by a barred window.

The cooperative itself is an entrepreneurship, employing some 33 people, including members of the Directive, some lower-level coordinators, security guards, and the electricity and water crew. The Tower can also be said to be a "job creator," providing opportunities for mototaxi drivers, grocery store owners and attendants, and building contractors hired by residents who lack the expertise to modify their premises on their own.

ARCHITECTURAL ANARCHY

Since virtually every family's living space is a work-in-progress, any observation is like a single frame of an endless film: today's makeshift partition may well be tomorrow's well-built, plastered, and painted wall. Moreover, there is considerable diversity of space-making among the "apartments" that Torre David's residents have designed and constructed for themselves, and living conditions range widely from slum-like settlements to middle- and even upper-middle-class environments. This is partly a function of the individuals involved—how recently they arrived, their talents and capacities, and their ambitions—and partly an issue of location. Since the 7th through the 16th floors of the high-rise were originally designed for a hotel, with access, formalized partitioning, and ventilation already in place, apartments there tend to be well-planned and developed. In contrast, rooms immediately above and surrounding the atrium, irregularly shaped spaces intended for commercial use, were built in haphazard fashion, irregularly divided, and even today lack brick or concrete walls.

The first and most significant architectural initiative undertaken by the residents was space-making itself. To that end, residents tended to begin with the most rudimentary of solutions: strings over which sheets or laundry are suspended; "walls" of boxes and furniture such as shelves and tall cabinets. There followed walls of red brick or cement block, temporarily stacked just a few courses high, without mortar. Eventually built up to 1.5 or 2 meters and mortared, the walls typically do not reach the slab above, but some residents have installed floating ceilings. Further refinements include sheet rock, stucco, and paint, as well as decorations. For ventilation, most residents rely on windows in the exterior walls, though some employ electric fans as well.

One particularly innovative resident scavenged computer cooling fans and installed them in his floating ceiling.

Interestingly, Torre David residents invest last, and least, in flooring, though some have installed linoleum or tile, and we saw the occasional rug. Generally, however, the concrete surface is left as is. In contrast, residents in barrios tend to focus their primary investments on well-constructed floors and roofs, the latter for weather protection, the former sealed against run-off and dirt.

During the day, residents rely almost exclusively on natural lighting. In the evenings and at night, they use a range of artificial lighting, from energy-guzzling incandescents to CFL and LED. The latter two are distributed by the Venezuelan government to barrio-dwellers free of charge, as a means of decreasing energy consumption. Nearly every household has a television, which, though technically not a lighting source, also provides illumination, especially the increasingly common large flat-screen sets. Mobile phones, too, are ubiquitous and afford the residents internet connection in a building lacking wifi networks and cable/dsl connections.

Photo: U-TT/Daniel Schwartz

INFRASTRUCTURE

Among the more obvious manifestations of cooperation and collaboration is Torre David's infrastructure which, however jury-rigged and jerry-built, is more stable and reliable than that which one finds in the hillside barrios. On the other hand, here, too, the residents have brought their priorities with them to Torre David.

SEWAGE AND GARBAGE

According to the residents, the underground parking level is often flooded with blackwater and rainwater, making it noisome and unfit for use. When the water rises to levels the residents consider unacceptable, they request help from the municipality, which sends a water pump truck to draw up much of the water. Some, however, always remains, and residents say—perhaps hyperbolically—that it would take 100 cistern trucks to fully empty the space, albeit on a temporary basis. Major modifications, beyond the capacity of the cooperative to undertake, would be required to render the basement impermeable to Caracas' recurring floods.

Intended for hotel use, the 7th through the 16th floors were equipped with sewage pipes, which the resident of those levels have tapped to create working sanitation systems. Using a bucket of water and gravity, some residents have flushing toilets that empty into the original system extending down through Torre David's central core and discharge mainly into the municipal sewage system.

In comparison to sewage disposal, garbage would seem a minor problem; but as the population of the complex continues to grow—and given Caracas' climate—it is an issue of continuing concern. Residents formerly disposed of household trash in a container located within the complex, but that inevitably attracted rats, compelling the cooperative to move the container half a block away. Each family is responsible for disposing of its own garbage.

At times, rainwater and blackwater accumulate in the
Tower's basement levels.

Photo (bottom): U-TT/Daniel Schwartz

WATER

The residents employ a rather Rube-Goldbergian system of water distribution, supplied from a city water main. Water is pumped up to the 11th floor of Edificio B and from there, using another pump, to the main 22 m³ water tank on the 16th floor of the high-rise. Yet another pump distributes water to the floors below and above; and another, on the 22nd floor, drives the water up to the 28th floor. The main tank, fed continually by one-inch PVC pipes, is located in the locked stairway, using a pre-existing three-sided space to which the residents added a fourth three-meter-high concrete wall. To monitor the water level, the floor manager climbs a homemade ladder and checks the tank with a flashlight.

Because the building lacks the piping infrastructure to serve each living space directly, residents have created a jury-rigged system: once a week the floor coordinators open each level of the locked stairway, where valves in the vertical supply pipe enable residents to plug in a hose, often of enormous length, from which they fill their own 500-liter water tanks, at least two per family. The water is not generally considered potable, so many residents boil it, supplementing this with purchases of 20-liter water jugs, ordered and paid for individually and delivered by a supplier.

Whereas in the early days of the occupation the water supply was adequate, usage has increased considerably, placing pressure on the system, as the average apartment now includes a toilet, sink, dishwasher, and washing machine. To date, the residents have incurred a debt of upwards of Bs. 510,000 (approx. US\$56,500) to HidroCapital, a matter of no great concern as the right to water service is guaranteed in Venezuela and thus the supply cannot be cut.

The main water tank on the 16th floor of Edificio A.   One of the Tower's water pumps.

Photos (left page): U·TT/Daniel Schwartz

WATER DISTRIBUTION

(1) Main water tank – level 16

Water for building a is pumped to and
distributed from the main water tank weekly

(2) Water pumps

(3) Apartment water tanks

Two 500 liter tanks per apartment (typical), refilled weekly

(4) City water main

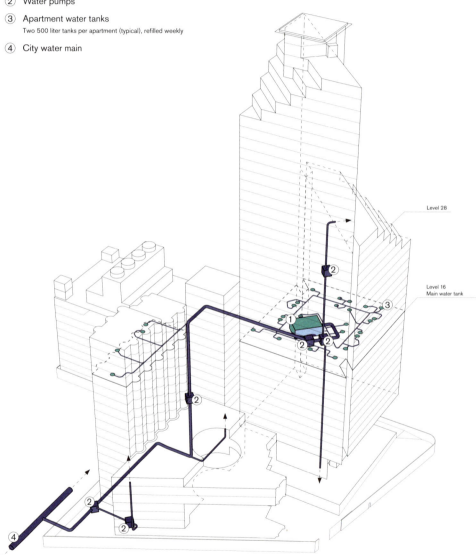

WATER DISTRIBUTION
Building A

Water hoses
—— Permanent supply hoses

- - - - Individual hoses

Water pumps
■ Floor 16–28

■ Floor 15–1

Water tanks

Main water tank
built by occupants

● Personal tanks
up to 500l

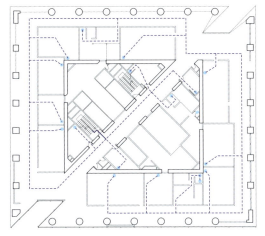

Floor 6

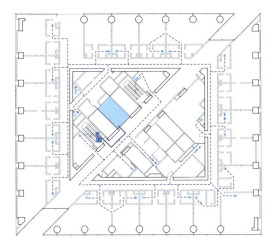

Floor 16

Some residents purchase drinking water from outside distributors to supplement the supply they receive from the Tower's centralized water system.

POWER

For residents of Torre David, electricity is critical to the structure's habitability, far more so than it is in the barrios: residents require it not only to power their appliances and devices, but to pump water and light the dangerous hallways and stairs. But electrifying the building has been a slow and problematic process. During the first invasion in 2003, squatters rigged a basic wire and switchbox that siphoned electricity from the city via a pole on the street. In 2007, at the beginning of the current invasion, the new occupants maintained that practice out of necessity, to cope with harsh conditions and in the absence of any formal management structure. Once the cooperative was fully established, a delegation approached Corpoelec (the state electricity institution) to formalize a contract that would provide more stable and consistent service. Doing so required that the cooperative first retire a debt of approximately US$10,000 incurred during the years of illicit access to the city power system.

The five-member electricity and water crew, working in alternating 12-hour shifts and supplied with two-way radios for constant communication, is responsible for power distribution and for uninterrupted monitoring of the system. Every several weeks, members of the crew will gather on a Saturday or Sunday and check important connections and repair any wires or switchboxes that may have been damaged through weather or wear and tear. The system and its maintenance are extraordinarily dangerous, and children are absolutely forbidden to remain in the vicinity while the crew works. The primary circuit boards are mounted on a homemade wooden box on the sixth floor and completely exposed to the elements.

Electricity for Torre David travels through four cables extending from Corpoelec's trunk cable into the building. Two of the cables were installed in an initial phase of electrification, the other two in a second installment. As of September 2012, the Cooperative is completing paperwork requesting a third

Main circuit board, 2011.

Main circuit board, 2012.

Photos: U-TT/Daniel Schwartz

phase, in which one thick cable would bring the electricity from the street into the Tower. The high-rise and Edificio B each have their own electrical system, but there is no electrical substation for the complex. Although the residents now enjoy a relatively steady and adequate power supply, on occasion a spike in demand overloads the grid and small fires break out, compelling the crew to change the main switches, at a cost of Bs. 3,000 (approximately US$350) each. The adequacy of the power supply is constantly at risk of compromise from increasing consumption, which currently totals 116,181.81 KwH per month for Torre David. It is worth noting that this level of usage is still just slightly more than half that of the average for the European Union and only one-third that of the average in Venezuela.

A reduction in demand would be an obvious, but nearly impossible solution, given the requirements for operating the water pumps and the preference among *caraqueños* of all socioeconomic strata to invest in tangible goods, an impulse that has driven an acquisitive, capitalistic instinct at odds with the culture of socialism.

The residents of Torre David, despite the precariousness of their economic well-being and, in part, because of the precariousness of the occupation, are no less inclined toward acquisition than any other *caraqueños.* In just one apartment, we inventoried two TV's, one DVD player, a refrigerator, a computer, a sound system, five lightbulbs, three cell phones, two ventilators, a hair drier, a drill, a washing machine, and a clothes iron. Not surprisingly, there are continual problems with internal connections, cables and switches that need constant repair, and uneven spikes in electricity usage.

Corpoelec is coordinating with representatives of Torre David on initiatives to repair and improve the flow of electricity, proposing specific breakers and types of connections for the electricity and water crew to implement. While Corpoelec does not work beyond the boundaries of a building site, as is typical of such utilities, it has in the past offered to undertake a major electrical project in the Tower, an offer residents rejected, citing the high cost. Corpoelec had also offered to pay 75 percent of the cost of such a project, but the April 2012 police raid on Torre David (mentioned in Chapter 1) has raised doubts as to whether the offer is still on the table.

ELECTRICITY DISTRIBUTION

① Building breakers

② Floor breakers

③ Apartment breakers

④ Consumption board

⑤ City electrical grid

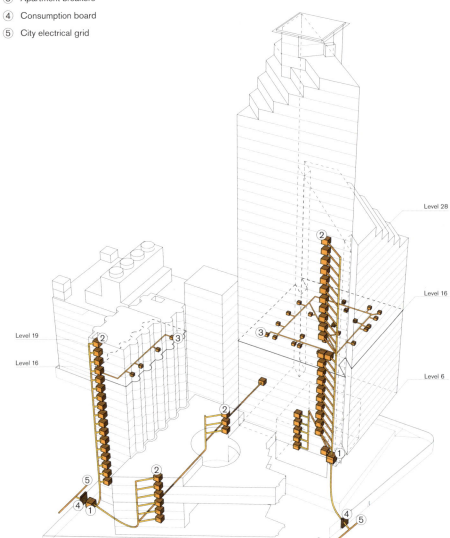

ELECTRICITY DISTRIBUTION
Building A

Cables
— Main cables
— Floor distribution
— Connection to personal breakers

Breakers
■ Main breakers
■ Secondary breakers
▪ Personal breakers

Water pumps
■ Floor 16–28
■ Floor 15–1

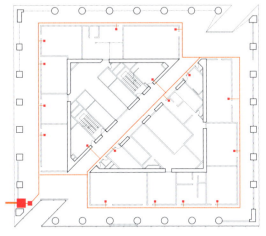

Floor 6

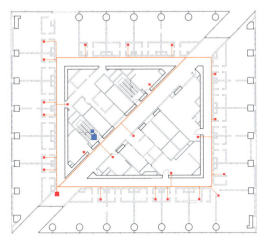

Floor 16

Found on one of the top floors are the unused
elevator motors and portions of the air conditioning
units. Some have been dismantled, and their
parts reused.

Like the stairwells, hallways have become
spaces for social interaction. Children often
play games and neighbors meet to chat in
the colorful corridors.

A group of workers build a new church for the
Tower on the ground floor of Edificio B.

235

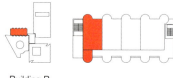

Building B
Level 8

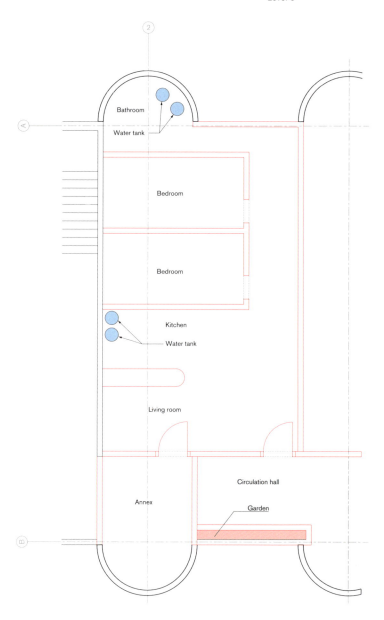

Bathroom

Water tank

Bedroom

Bedroom

Kitchen

Water tank

Living room

Circulation hall

Garden

Annex

Floor plan

0   1   2

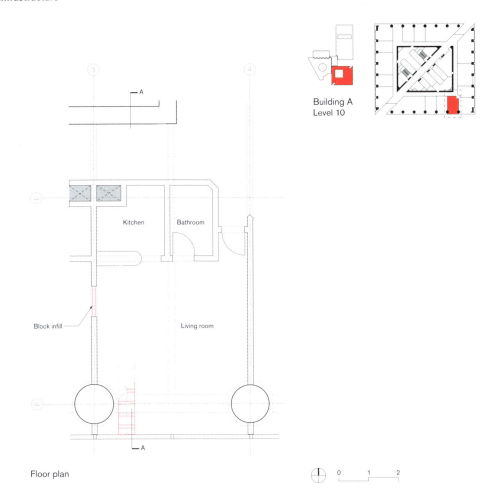

Building A
Level 10

Kitchen

Bathroom

Block infill

Living room

Floor plan

0   1   2

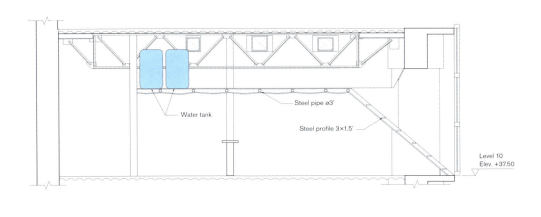

Water tank

Steel pipe ø3'

Steel profile 3×1.5'

Level 10
Elev. +37.50

Section A-A

0   1   2

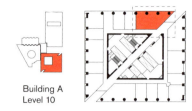

Building A
Level 10

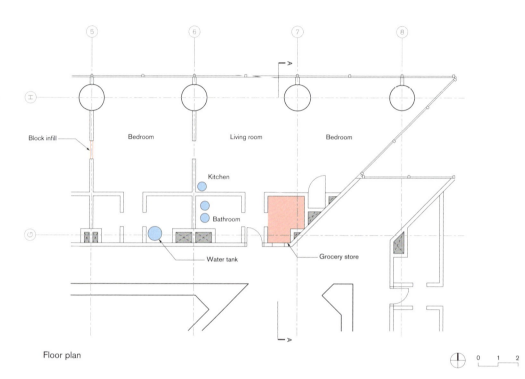

Block infill

Bedroom

Living room

Bedroom

Kitchen

Bathroom

Water tank

Grocery store

Floor plan

0   1   2

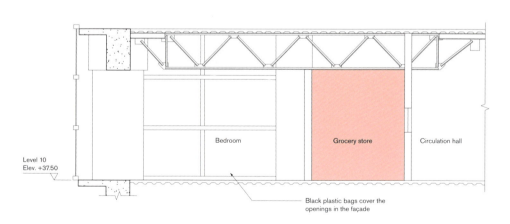

Level 10
Elev. +37.50

Bedroom

Grocery store

Circulation hall

Black plastic bags cover the
openings in the façade

Section A-A

0   1   2

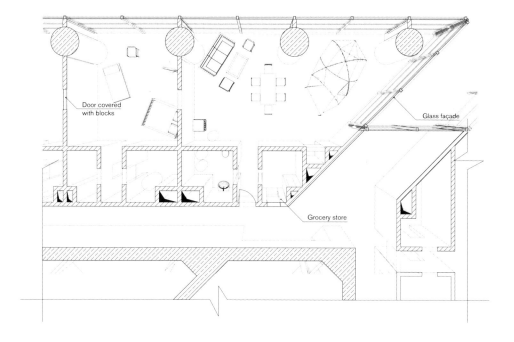

Door covered
with blocks

Glass façade

Grocery store

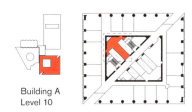

Building A
Level 10

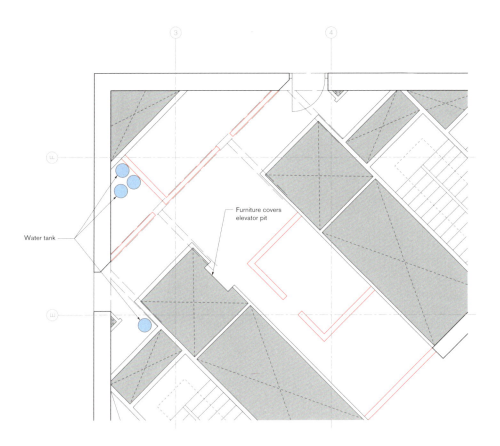

Water tank

Furniture covers
elevator pit

Floor plan

0   1   2

Infrastructure

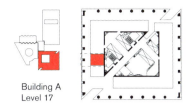

Building A
Level 17

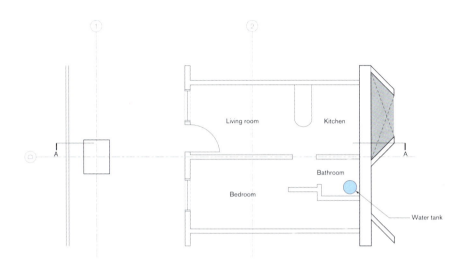

Living room

Kitchen

A

A

Bathroom

Bedroom

Water tank

Floor plan

0   1   2

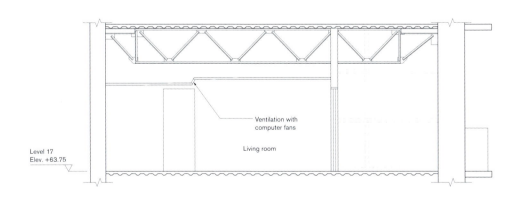

Ventilation with
computer fans

Living room

Level 17
Elev. +63.75

Section A-A

0   1   2

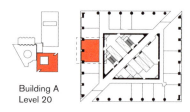

Building A
Level 20

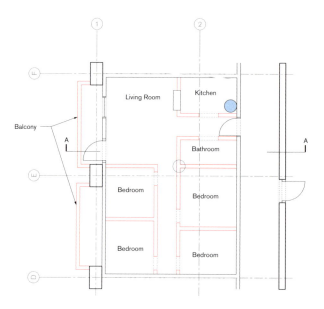

Living Room

Kitchen

Balcony

Bathroom

Bedroom

Bedroom

Bedroom

Bedroom

A

A

Floor plan

0   1   2

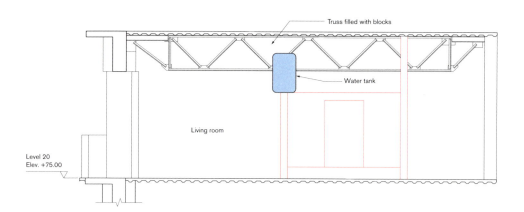

Truss filled with blocks

Water tank

Living room

Level 20
Elev. +75.00

Section A-A

0   1   2

Infrastructure

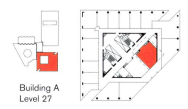

Building A
Level 27

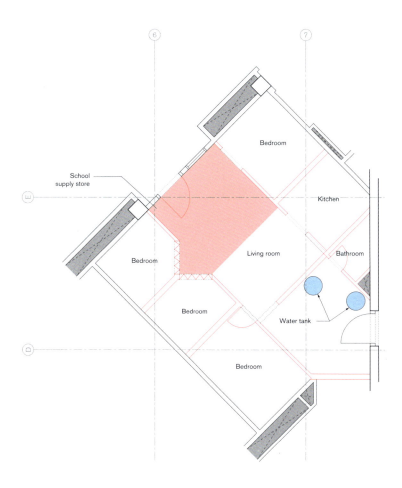

School
supply store

Bedroom

Kitchen

Bedroom

Living room

Bathroom

Bedroom

Water tank

Bedroom

Floor plan

Already equipped with a roof over their heads, new residents in essence need little else to begin living in Torre David. A tent or a few sheets are enough to create a private space.

As residents build walls to define their individual
spaces, some add stucco, changing the appearance
and atmosphere of the rooms they have created.

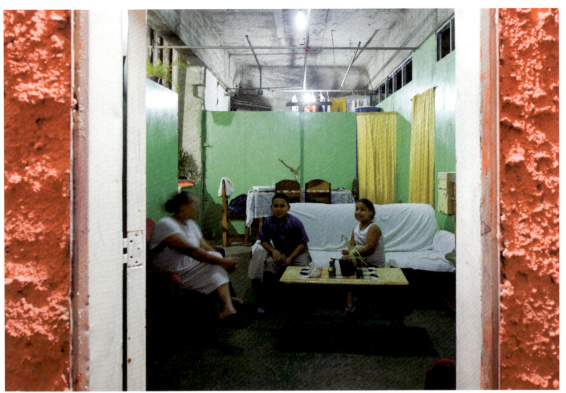

While some residents leave their walls as bare
bricks, others prefer to decorate their homes with
various types of wall coverings.

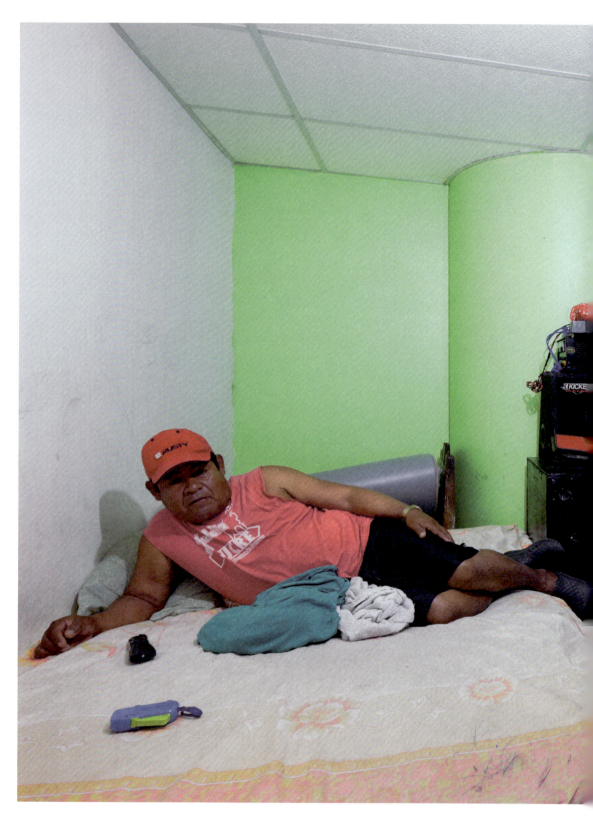

In 2007, at age 92, this woman was carried up to her
20th-floor apartment where she now lives with her children
and grandchildren. She has not left her floor, not to
mention the building, in the five years since she moved in.

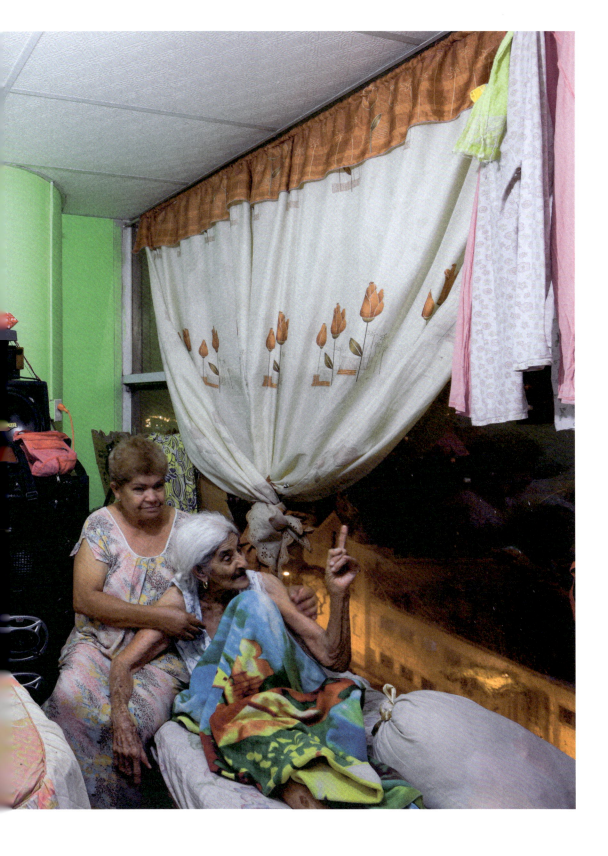

From ceramic tiled walls to an elephant trophy
centerpiece, residents have used all manner
of materials and found objects to decorate their
spaces.

Residents are often inventive in their use
of space. This family has built an extra
floor inside their apartment to maximize
their living area.

Resident Gladys Flores has used a full façade panel and elevator springs to build a table for her home.

Residents throw a birthday party, decorating
the space with festive balloons and a Spiderman
piñata.

The church in Edificio B has a devout group
of followers; sermons and prayers are
sometimes projected throughout the complex
over loudspeakers.

From hair salons and tailor ateliers to grocery
stores and a community gym, residents have set
up a variety of small businesses and community
spaces throughout Torre David.

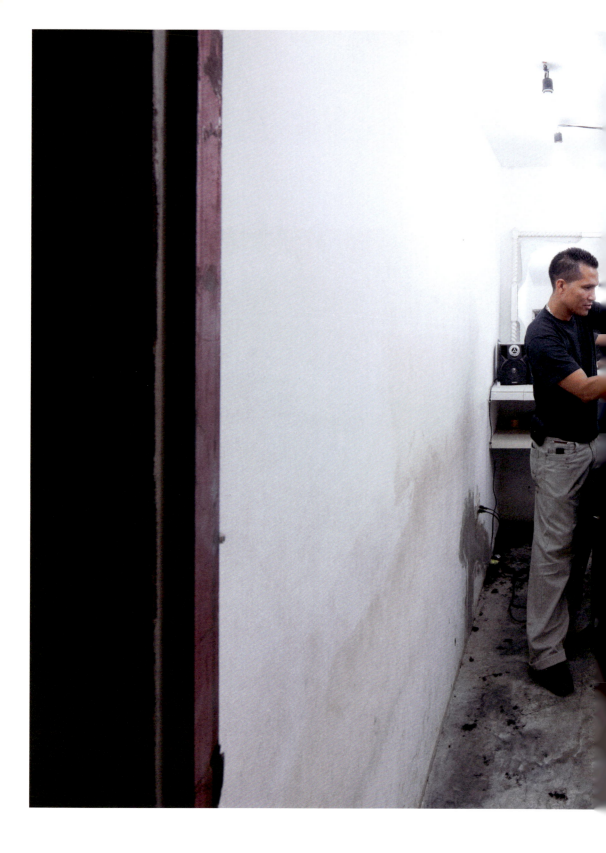

By breaking through various walls, residents have
created new pathways for movement throughout
the complex.

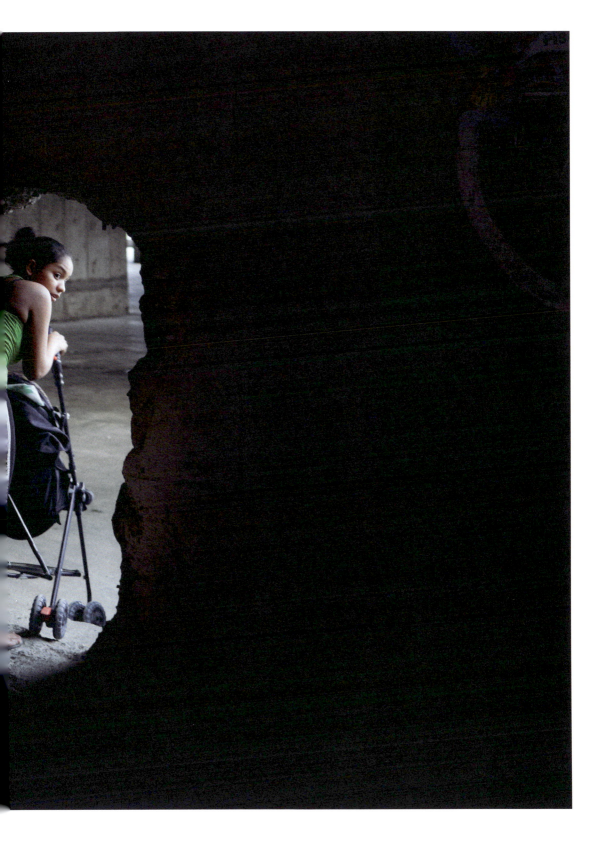

Some residents have built their individual homes between the concrete columns of Edificio A and the atrium.

Designed as the complex's main entrance, the atrium has since been repurposed as a space for community meetings as well as a growing number of individual apartments.

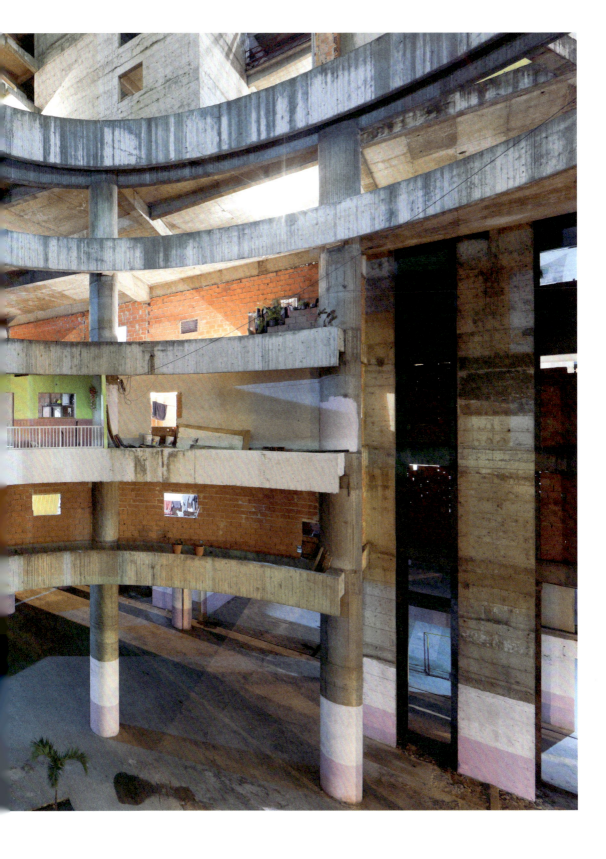

The top floors remain unoccupied, appearing
much as they did when residents first moved into
the tower in 2007.

Come nightfall, the diversity of the apartments and the residents' individual lighting and décor choices become even more apparent.

WHAT EXACTLY IS TORRE DAVID?

Having examined Torre David closely and intensively, in this snapshot in time, perhaps we can now begin to look for answers to some of the questions it raises. Clearly, as Andres Lepik explains in the introduction, it does not meet the conventional criteria for a slum, vertical or otherwise. Neither does it meet the equally conventional standards for a residential high-rise. It would seem to partake of both, as well as its own, singular category of urban development.

In some respects, one can see Torre David's antecedents in the barrios: make-shift solutions in the absence of an infrastructure in the high-rise, in the absence of municipal services in the barrios; the use of bricks and found materials in both; certain elements of the architectural vernacular, such as arched doorways and interior windows and pass-throughs. Certain customs or habits persist, too. Some readers may be shocked at the absence of safety measures in Torre David, particularly those that would protect children; and, indeed, there has been more than one death resulting from a terrible fall from an unenclosed opening in the building's exterior. But the hillside barrios are at least as dangerous; and, as one resident explained, children are taught—and expected—to be careful of their surroundings.

Despite the precariousness of the occupation and because Torre David is structurally strong and durable, one sees in the construction of many of the family apartments a greater striving for permanence and a different kind of aspiration. It would seem that the physical fragility of the barrios—given their construction and exposure to mudslides, and their extreme population density—are greater obstacles to a sense of ownership than Torre David's tenuous occupancy. And while the living quarters in the latter are, like the barrio dwellings, in an ongoing state of creation, expansion, and enhancement, many of the Torre David residents are explicitly and purposefully moving toward a middle-class lifestyle.

One of the foundational elements of Torre David is surely the nature of its community. The common ground consists of more than the religious affiliation of the residents: it is built, too, on shared purpose. In this respect, the community of Torre David is forward-looking. It represents less an explicit statement about the failures of an administration than a continual striving for a better quality of life. Unlike some of the communes of the 1960s, it did not have its origins in a rebellion or protest against a regime or way of life; such collectives often collapse when the status quo of the "real world" changes, personal imperatives intervene, or, in the absence of a clear purpose, stagnation sets in.

What these communes lacked, and the residents of Torre David evidence clearly, is an ongoing engagement with the society in which they live and an impulse toward improvement of their lives. This, in turn, seems intimately associated with continual development and growth. The architecture practiced by the residents defies the conventional assumptions about the purposes and ends of design; it constantly evolves, adapting to an ever-moving present. In that respect, Torre David is a microcosm of the mega-city itself, in which the influx of great numbers of people and the growth of the informal, as represented by the barrios, chip away at and erode the carefully mapped urban plan.

There are no "starchitects" in Torre David—technically, there are no architects of any sort. The residents, unencumbered by "principles of design," theories of aesthetics, or the received wisdom of the past, build what makes sense to them, what suits their purposes and personalities. They are untroubled by revision and informality and, equally, by the notion of incremental development and improvement.

If this is the future—if Torre David is the informal city writ small—architects and urban planners face a major challenge: who and what are we to those we serve? What, exactly, are we designing, and to what end? For that matter, what can we bring to Torre David that offers the best of our professional skill and expertise and also respects and sustains the healthy informality of the community's development?

"Look, what's important here is that after we do this work we have to go floor by floor to talk to the whole community and explain to them that we must be aware of energy consumption. We need to lower consumption because demand is too high and the amperage is too high."

—Jorge Morales, head electrician and resident of Torre David

III: POSS

What then shall we do?[1]

It used to be said that the only certain things in life are death and taxes. Now, in the early 21st century, it is a given that among life's certainties is rapid and unpredictable change.

The world's mega-cities are in a constant and dramatic state of flux. Buildings are demolished; new ones are erected. Economies rise and fall. Social and political order are whimsical, leaders are capricious. People flood in from the countryside, from other countries, looking for work, shelter, security. What of buildings? No one who designs, or constructs, or pays for the design and construction of a building wants to think of it as evanescent or mutable. And yet that is precisely what we must have in mind when we design and build.

In such an infinitely unstable environment, architects must throw away their Ruskin—"When we build, let us think that we build forever"[2]—in favor of new goals: resilience, adaptability, and transformability. Resilience is the capacity of a building or a system to absorb change *in medias res* without resisting it; adaptability relates to the components and their influence on resilience over time; and transformability is that which enables survival.

Torre David's physical structure and the needs of its occupants are clearly at odds. While the extreme verticality is accompanied by the kind of density we recognize as valuable for certain kinds of efficiencies and for a desirable social concentration, it also constrains the residents' spatial mobility. As the British architect and urbanist Peter Land notes:

> [T]he negative consequences for low-income families living in apartments in high-rise structures, disconnected from the ground, is now well-known. Also, the density advantages are minimal when cost, maintenance, access, privacy, human scale, and the frequent impossibility of unit expansion are considered.[3]

1 The translated title of a non-fiction work by Leo Tolstoy, in which he describes the social, economic, and political conditions in 19th-century Russia and the urgent need for action.

2 John Ruskin, *The Seven Lamps of Architecture*, Ch. VI: "The Lamp of Memory."

3 Peter Land, interview by Daniel Schwartz, May 24, 2012. In Newark, New Jersey, the consequences were evident as far back as 25 years ago, when the city demolished the Scudder Homes, a housing project roiled by rent strikes, vandalism, and poor maintenance. In 2010, the city tore down the infamous Douglass-Harrison Homes, which had become an open-air drug and prostitution market ignored

IBILITY

The residents of Torre David have managed to defy Land's analysis with respect to unit expansion and modification; and, in defiance of the physical limitations of the building, they have fostered a remarkable degree of social exchange, evident in the disciplined leadership structure, democratic processes, and religious bonds. Despite the insecurity of their habitation, they continue to modify their spaces, improving them to fit the needs of the community and to reach continually for a better standard of living. That impulse is inherent in all human placemaking, throughout history, but we know of no other example quite so singular or so capable of exciting the architectural imagination. As a laboratory, or zone of experimentation, Torre David challenged us to conceive new technical retrofits and structural solutions that can enhance the safety, functionality, and social vibrancy of the space.

by the police. That same year, Chicago demolished the 68-year-old Cabrini-Green projects, the site of a gang war that killed 11 residents in three months. See Camilo José Vergara's *The New American Ghetto* (New Brunswick, NJ: Rutgers University Press, 1995).

OBJECTIVES

Our vision arises from the premise of sustainability as the only practical and ethical basis on which to build and grow. Conventional concepts of sustainable architecture, of course, do not readily apply to the circumstances of Torre David. Even in the context of the retrofitting or adaptive reuse of existing buildings, and certainly in regard to new structures, we typically design for a reduction of energy consumption, a smaller carbon footprint, self-sufficiency of the structure itself—anything, in other words, that will mitigate the impact of our designs on the environment, as well as improve the health and well-being of the users. This last is of vital importance in our approach to sustainability for Torre David; but the environmental impact of the building and of its use is negligible, and the reduction of energy consumption is not, thus far, an urgent goal.

The interventions we explored during this project and present as possible approaches in this chapter are aimed at raising the standard of living for the residents of Torre David, while minimizing the demands on Caracas' already overtaxed power grid (reliant, as we noted earlier, on hydroelectricity from the Guri Dam) and on non-renewable resources, capitalizing on renewable resources, and—not least—taking into account the social and economic issues that are inextricable from any notion of "sustainability" in the context of Torre David. Any intervention we considered also had to be organic, in the sense of enabling and requiring the direct participation of the residents. Sustainability, in any context, is not merely an issue of architectural and engineering design and of technology, but of operations and behaviors.

We also considered the physical appearance of the building, both because the residents have indicated its importance to them and because an improved outward aspect would help integrate the community into the social and economic fabric of the city by compelling outsiders to reconsider their perceptions and preconceptions of the residents.

THE STATUS QUO

The residents of Torre David, by nature and constraint, are comparatively parsimonious in their use of resources. To some extent, they have little choice: during dry seasons and periods of high demand, the hydroelectric installation at Guri Dam, which generates two-thirds of the electricity for Caracas, runs out of capacity. The overall demand for electricity cannot be met, and the city's supply of fresh water is limited. Moreover, as we noted in the previous chapter, Torre David has a limited pumping and distribution system that operates only one or two times a week. The infrastructure for electricity has similar deficiencies: the connection to the local grid is susceptible to overloading and loses capacity during peak periods.[4]

At present, water consumption on a per-family basis—about 3.6 m³ a month—is just one-third of the regional average and one-fourth the European average.[5] Those comparisons hold true for electrical usage as well—just 155 kWh monthly per family. While the number of energy-consuming appliances is lower among Torre David residents than among higher-income families, as one would expect, the lower consumption is also due to the almost total absence

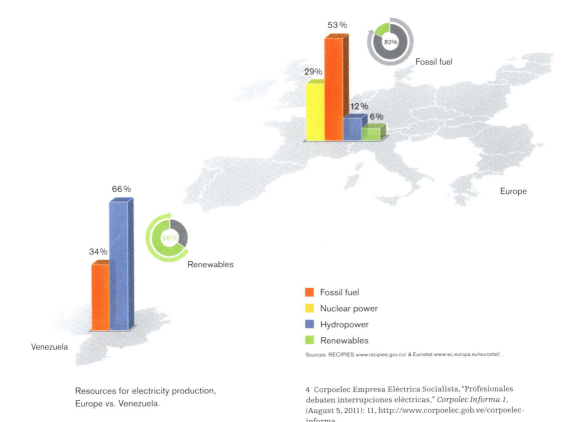

Resources for electricity production, Europe vs. Venezuela.

4 Corpoelec Empresa Eléctrica Socialista, "Profesionales debaten interrupciones eléctricas," *Corpolec Informa 1,* (August 5, 2011): 11, http://www.corpoelec.gob.ve/corpoelec-informa.
5 Ministerio del Poder Popular para la Energía Electrica, www.mppee.gob.ve/; ODYSSEE, www.odyssee-indicators.org; Eurostat, www.ec.europa.edu/eurostat.

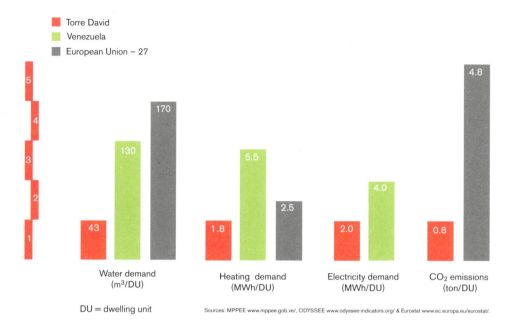

Resources consumption per year, Europe vs. Venezuela and Torre David.

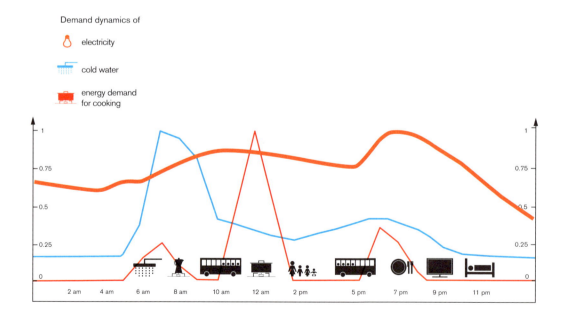

Peaks and dynamics of resource consumption.

of HVAC equipment. For cooking purposes and domestic hot water, residents use propane or butane. This last is responsible for 60 percent of Torre David's total emissions, which are equivalent to just half the regional average.

As is generally true in urban areas, the demand for water and power in Torre David fluctuates across the day. Water consumption peaks twice a day, in the morning—between 6am and 8am—and again between 6pm and 8pm in the evening; these two peak demand periods account for 41 percent of the total demand for water. Electrical usage also peaks twice a day, but for longer periods—9am to 12pm and 6pm to 9pm—which account for 38 percent of the total consumption.

This analysis leads us to several objectives. The fluctuations in demand and the concomitant failure of the grid to supply adequate power during peak periods should be addressed by the use of one or more renewable resources—in this case solar and/or wind. There must also be the means to store electricity to mitigate the intermittency of those resources. All possibilities for reducing demand should be explored. And any systems and procedures for the supply of and demand for water and electricity must be decentralized and transparent to the users, so that they become invested in prudent use and ongoing maintenance.

EVALUATION OF OPTIONS

As we have noted, two-thirds of the demand for electricity is met by the power grid, supplied by the hydroelectric plant. But that supply often falls short during peak periods. The location and massing of Torre David suggest at least two opportunities for harvesting renewable energy resources.

Solar power would seem an obvious choice, given Caracas' location close to the equator. However, this is of limited suitability for generating power because of issues of location, technologies, and architecture. Caracas suffers from frequent overcast conditions; and the massing of the Torre David complex offers insufficient horizontal surfaces.

On the other hand, Torre David, at a height of around 170 meters, has extensive vertical surfaces unshielded by any adjacent structure, a situation that lends itself to harvesting wind energy. The northern and eastern façades in particular are exposed to the prevailing winds, which generally blow some 70 percent of the time. Moreover, in contrast to solar energy harvesting, wind power can be captured by simple, low-cost technologies, which are readily accessible to the users and require far less maintenance.

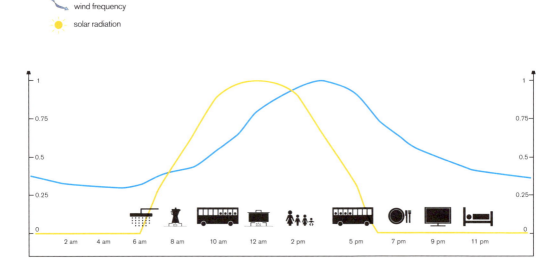

Dynamics of solar radiation and prevailing winds.

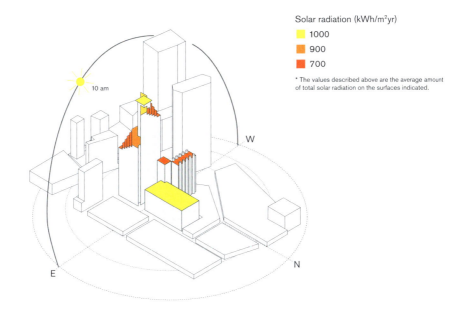

Solar radiation (kWh/m²yr)

- 1000
- 900
- 700

* The values described above are the average amount of total solar radiation on the surfaces indicated.

W

E

N

10 am

Solar radiation on horizontal surfaces.

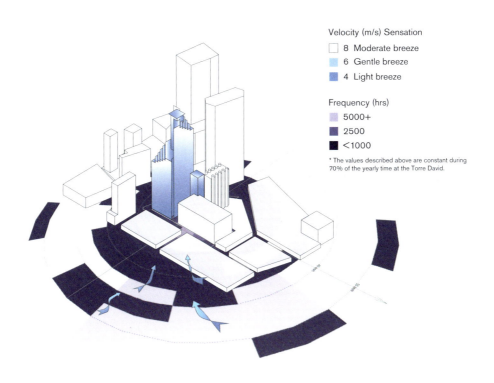

Velocity (m/s) Sensation

- 8 Moderate breeze
- 6 Gentle breeze
- 4 Light breeze

Frequency (hrs)

- 5000+
- 2500
- <1000

* The values described above are constant during 70% of the yearly time at the Torre David.

Prevailing winds.

SOLUTIONS

HARNESSING NATURE

Our approach to addressing electricity production and use in Torre David is two-fold, employing both wind turbines and a revolutionary pumped pico hydro storage system. We believe that in using the two technologies in a complementary manner, Torre David could generate and store electricity at low cost and with minimal complexity.

In the simplest terms, arrays of wind turbines placed on the upper portions of Torre David's east façade would generate electricity during the day. The turbines would be structured as racks of eight small pinion-shaped horizontal axis wind propellers, with a 25-centimeter diameter, interlocked horizontally. Located on the façade, they would only reduce air circulation into the high-rise by 30 percent, pose no safety threat to residents using internal spaces, and generate only a slight increase in noise pollution compared to the existing levels of sound produced by home appliances and street traffic. The electricity produced by these turbines, available at times of high wind energy and low demand, would primarily be used to pump water up to a series of

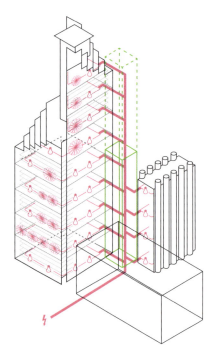

Concept for electricity generation and infrastructure.

reservoirs located at different levels within Edificio K. This water, meant for distribution and consumption, would also be instrumental in the pumped pico hydro system, which uses the potential energy of the stored water to generate electricity. In releasing the stored water during times of high electricity demand, the falling water's gravitational force drives a series of pico hydro turbines located below occupied levels, thus generating electricity.

This combination of technologies, implemented in a vertical manner to serve the needs of a large population, is without precedent. It is a system that is capable of producing approximately 24 percent of Torre David's electricity, though it would likely require experimentation and monitoring to derive and sustain efficient usage. With a computerized control station, and initial expert monitoring and training, we believe that residents would be able to operate and improve upon the system over time as electricity demand rises.

At the same time that we devised systems to ensure consistent and adequate supply, we also looked at the possibility of reducing demand. Although this is a vital goal for the longer term, as it engenders a conservative attitude toward sustainability in general, it is likely to have only a minimal impact on Torre David. Electricity is not an issue in heating, as Venezuela has very large reserves of natural and butane gas, and use of these is heavily promoted by

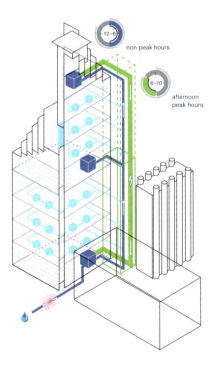

Water supply and energy storage.

the government through financing and subsidies. As for electrical appliances, the residents have, in recent years, introduced more energy-efficient models; but high-consumption lighting still uses 20 percent of the electricity. The replacement of incandescent bulbs with the newer, highly efficient bulbs could reduce demand by 10 percent.

It should be noted that any feasible and efficiency-producing interventions must not only address current demand, but also be sufficiently flexible and adaptable to meet future needs. Should the residents of Torre David succeed in remaining *in situ,* they will surely continue to improve their standard of living. It would be unwise to assume that those who are at present without a dishwasher, for instance, will never acquire one. A stable supply of electricity may encourage higher usage. The installation of some form of vertical transportation will result in greater demand for power. Nothing about Torre David is ever static.

A TRANSPORTATION BALANCING ACT

Indeed, the residents are constantly on the move—but their vertical mobility is severely curtailed by the absence of some form of mechanical transportation. Climbing the stairs is onerous even for the young and healthy; it is dangerous for small children and impossible for the very elderly and the infirm. Moreover, the residents' ability to continue building and modifying their living spaces is considerably slowed by the need to carry materials up many flights of stairs.

The standard solution, a bank of elevators, is impractical, not only because of the up-front costs, but also considering two key objectives of any intervention. Elevators require considerable power—more than would be prudent given the goal of relying primarily on the on-site generation of electricity. And the complexity of the system would defeat the aim of enabling the residents to install, operate, and maintain their own facilities and amenities.

If, instead of thinking of Torre David as a conventional high-rise, it is conceived as a vertical city, then vertical transportation becomes the equivalent of a bus line, whose operation, instead of being continually available and constantly functioning, is scheduled on an as-needed basis. The "route" would be a proposed vertical extension of Edificio K, which would also serve to supply electricity and water, making it an infrastructure backbone—in effect, a traditional building core.

The system would operate by balancing the incoming (ascending) load with the outgoing (descending) load, both comprised of passengers, goods, construction materials, and—in the case of the latter—waste. While conventional

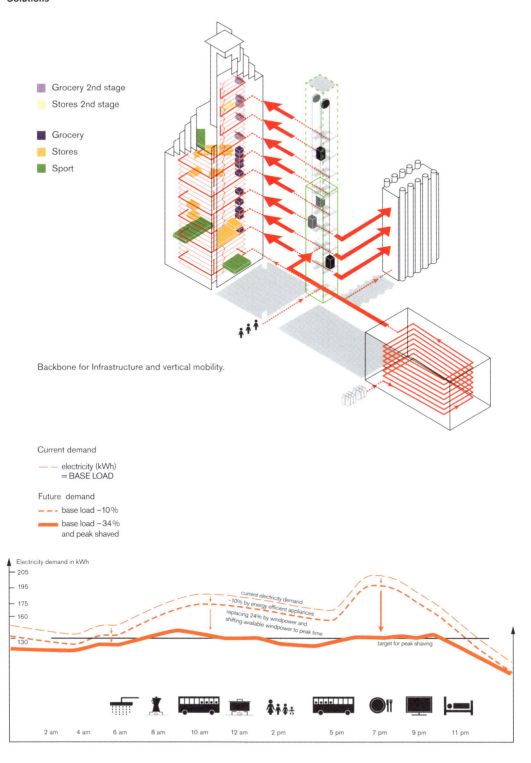

Grocery 2nd stage
Stores 2nd stage

Grocery
Stores
Sport

Backbone for Infrastructure and vertical mobility.

Current demand

— — electricity (kWh)
= BASE LOAD

Future demand

– – – base load −10%

▬▬▬ base load −34%
and peak shaved

Electricity demand in kWh

205
195
175
160

130

current electricity demand
−10% by energy efficient appliances
replacing 24% by windpower and
shifting available windpower to peak time

target for peak shaving

| 2 am | 4 am | 6 am | 8 am | 10 am | 12 am | 2 pm | 5 pm | 7 pm | 9 pm | 11 pm |

Measures combined: demand reduction and peak shaving.

elevator systems also use this counterweight principle, they rely heavily on electricity to balance the frequently unequal weight of the two major components. The bus system, in contrast, relies upon an equivalence of ascending and descending elements and therefore requires very little additional energy.

The bus does, however, require the kind of efficient coordination, communication, and work groups for which the residents of Torre David have already organized themselves. A timetable for the system's operation would take into account peak travel times—morning and evening "rush hours," in effect—coordinating these with the transportation of goods and materials in the morning and with waste disposal and sports or other activities in the evenings. During off-peak hours, if there is inadequate counterweight available, the bus can be driven by electricity stored in batteries and generated either by wind power or by the descent of the cab.

Taking a city bus line, once again, as the model, the vertical bus would not stop at every floor, but every five floors, a distance that meets the minimum accessibility in multistory buildings.[6] Each stop would manage the flow of the three floors below and two above; residents would use the stairs to cover the intervals, which would preserve the social interactions that help foster cohesiveness and cordiality.

6 Terry Patterson, *Illustrated 2009 Building Code Handbook* (New York: McGraw-Hill Professional, 2009).

ARCHITECTURAL INTERVENTION

The installation of the wind harvesting system on the façades of Torre David offers an opportunity to improve on the aesthetics as well. The external bracing system that would hold the wind turbines might also be used, in neutral spaces, to support a type of curtain wall structure with panels of varying color and texture, thus harmonizing the façade and eliminating the improvised and shoddy appearance. A new façade treatment can also address the safety issues resulting from open and unguarded portions of the exterior. And integrating the various entrances and the guard positions into an overall aesthetic would create a more neighborly and less threatening relationship with the surroundings. In addition, the extension of Edificio K and its use as the core for vertical circulation of people and systems could be given transparency, which makes for visual liveliness and interest, as well as "normalizing" the residents and their activities in the eyes of passersby.

Such interventions would necessarily be implemented in phases, making a gradual, step-by-step transition and enabling the residents to continue to invest "sweat-equity" in Torre David. Phase 1 would involve the installation of the wind power system on the eastern façade and the construction of the pico hydro system, both of which would provide immediate benefits. In Phase 2, Edificio K would be extended, expanding the wind power system and/or enabling the occupancy of higher floors of Torre David.

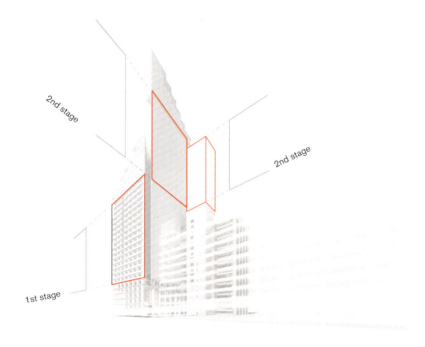

Realization stages.

Intervention at the east and north façade.

Intervention at the main tower façade.

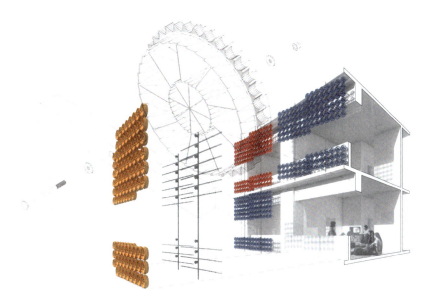

Façade detail of the wind energy system.

OBSERVATIONS AND LESSONS

Like many—perhaps most—architects, urbanists, and land-use planners, we have focused particular attention on the issue of sustainability, surely among the most pressing of contemporary concerns. It is also abundantly clear that, as valuable as Torre David is as a laboratory for the real-world testing of various approaches to sustainable design and operations, Venezuela itself is unlikely to see a significant move toward sustainable architecture in the foreseeable future. Government subsidies make oil and natural gas inexpensive in themselves and in comparison with other, renewable resources. Moreover, Caracas draws its power supply from hydro-electricity, an alternative and renewable source. Other countries, however, are actively pursuing various sustainable and carbon-neutral solutions. For them, for their literally and figuratively homeless populations, and for the professionals who practice in their mega-cities, Torre David may well produce widely applicable means and methods for achieving their goals.

Our experience at Torre David also illustrates the vital importance of extending the meaning of sustainability to include enabling the end-users to sustain the operations and maintenance of any intervention through their own initiative and efforts. Of course, Torre David has an unusually cohesive and relatively homogeneous population, setting it apart from other squats. But ensuring that residents can and will take effective ownership of a property, however extra-legally occupied, seems to us essential for continuing livability and viability. For the anti-model, one has only to look at many North American housing projects: financed, designed, built, and—theoretically—maintained by public agencies, all with the best intentions; but eventually subject to neglect and deterioration.

This is by no means to suggest that the residents of Torre David and of similar properties would ideally be left entirely on their own. Clearly they can benefit from innovative technologies developed by others, particularly private enterprises with strong research initiatives. Indeed, Torre David affords architects and engineers a valuable context in which to test solutions that may prove appropriate for other projects in other parts of the world. The involvement of the Schindler Group in exploring alternatives to the conventional elevator is a case in point. For them—and, we hope, for other companies that develop and manufacture lighting, ventilation, security, plumbing, and other essential systems and fixtures—Torre David provides a setting for testing innovative solutions. It is a highly efficient laboratory, given its capacity to provide quick reactions and responses, revealing drawbacks or problems and enabling their on-site correction. Rather than waiting for the marketplace to reveal the inadequacies of a new solution and, at best, having to issue a recall or, at worst, having their reputations and bottom-line both eroded, private companies can take a system or product swiftly through development and enter the market with a proven solution.

The fact that Torre David is, as we have noted before, a continually changing, evolving organism is perhaps its least unexpected feature. The "growing building" is a phenomenon we have observed throughout our exploration of the informal, not only in Caracas but also in other mega-cities. The only truly static element in Torre David is the concrete structure—everything else is in flux. The process of perpetual change makes Torre David singularly useful as a framework from which the future of urban architecture can emerge.

On the 28th floor of the high-rise, brothers
Grabiel and Frankenstein, along with their friend
Deivis, have built this community gym from
scrap materials such as pulleys taken from the

abandoned elevators. The gym is open to
all Torre David residents.

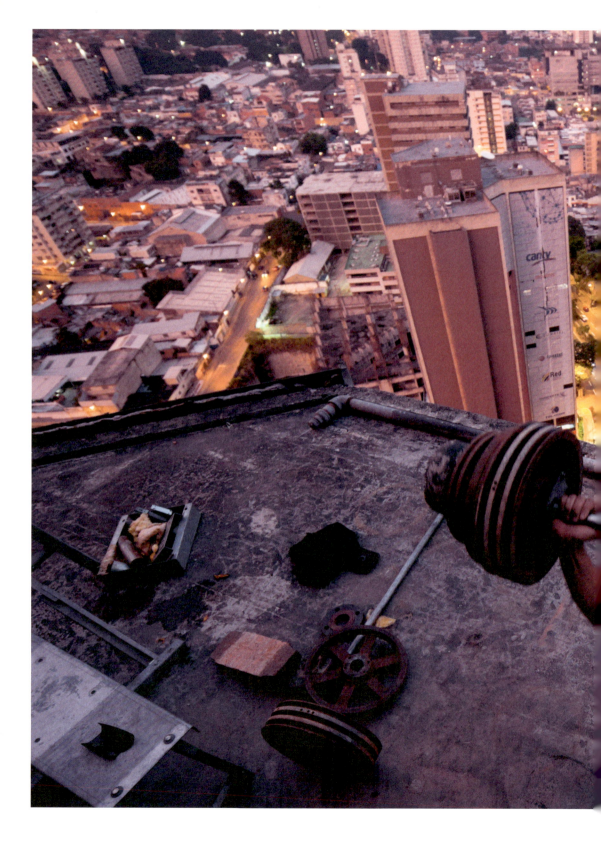

"If the government came and worked with us and saw what we did, if we could work together in collaboration, that would be exceptional—it would be a transformation. And we would demonstrate to the whole world that a community of humble people is capable of a masterpiece."

—Gladys Flores, Secretary of the Asociacion Cooperativa de Vivienda "Casiques de Venezuela," R.L.

IV: POTE

NTIAL

Everything that rises must converge.[1]

We can easily imagine two very different but equally inappropriate and un-helpful reactions to Torre David. One comes from within the architectural establishment, which is appalled to see what has befallen Enrique Gómez's design, dismayed by the conditions in which the residents live, and wants immediately to set about designing both a new high-rise and "better" hous-ing for the poor. That response arises from the conviction that solutions lie in the traditions of architecture and urban planning. The other comes from the architectural anti-establishment, those who believe the first group are out of touch, who reject everything their architectural training has taught them, but who also want to design "better" housing.

Both are right. Both are wrong. Both are equally conventional and equally "liberal" in their desire to use architecture as the means to improve lives and the quality of life for the world's poorest. Their impulses are ideological, not practical, in origin. The problem, as we see it, is that these arise from 20th-century notions of what a city is, who inhabits it, and where it is going. They are either/or, us/them approaches to problem solving. In the 21st century, what we need is both/and.

Torre David should neither be romanticized nor scorned; it has provided us with valuable lessons, but it is not an object lesson.

1 Pierre Teilhard de Chardin, *Building the Earth and the Psychological Conditions of Human Unification* (New York: Avon Books, 1969). In full, de Chardin, a French Jesuit and philosopher, writes: "Remain true to yourself, but move ever upward toward greater consciousness and greater love! At the summit you will find yourselves united with all those who, from every direction, have make the same ascent. For everything that rises must converge."

WHAT SHOULD WE CALL THIS THING?

As we investigated Torre David, we found ourselves unavoidably considering the various philosophies into which it might fall. Though the project resisted absolute categorization, the analytic process was useful in refining our thinking.

Initially, Torre David seemed a paradigm of Foucault's heterotopia. That is, he defines heterotopias as places "that have the curious property of being in relation with all the other sites, but in such a way as to suspect, neutralize, and invert the set of relations that they happen to designate, mirror, or reflect."[2] These are spaces that have more layers of meaning or relationships to other spaces than immediately meet the eye; they have the capacity to affirm difference and to afford the means of escape from authoritarianism and repression.

It was a compelling perspective. Torre David is a literal refuge from homelessness for hundreds of families and a figurative advertisement for alternative modes of housing. Its leadership has shaped a place where alternative social and political models exist simultaneously, both rhetorically and practically. It defies the ambiguity of the Chávez government's approach to property: the law, or rhetoric, asserts rights of ownership, but in practice the administration encourages appropriation. And it does so by seeking legal ownership rights while engaging in an extra-legal occupation. And just as Foucault cherished heterotopias for their capacity to provide society with "reserves of imagination," we were captivated by Torre David's spatial implications and potential.

Eventually, however, we found heterotopia too dependent on an understanding of urban spaces as static. The concept presumes a rigid and, most reductively, binary notion of society. Even Foucault recognized the limitations of his thesis as an analytical tool and abandoned it shortly after its initial presentation.

Other ways of understanding—if not precisely naming—Torre David proved more enlightening. Edward Soja tells us that Thirdspace is "an-Other way of understanding and acting to change the spatiality of human life, a distinct mode of critical spatial awareness that is appropriate to the new scope and significance being brought about in the rebalanced trialectics of spatiality-historicality-sociality."[3] While Soja acknowledges the persistence of duality, he brings the polar opposites together in Thirdspace, where "everything comes together... subjectivity and objectivity, the abstract and the concrete, the real and the imagined, the knowable and the unimaginable, the repetitive and the differential, structure and agency, mind and body, consciousness and the

2 Michel Foucault, "Des espaces autres." Written in 1967, but not published until the October 1984 issue of *Architecture, Mouvement, Continuité*, n. 5, pp. 46–49.
3 Edward Soja, Thirdspace (Malden, MA: Blackwell Publishers, 1996), 57.
4 Ibid.

5 Henri Lefebvre, *The Production of Space*, trans. Donald Nicholson-Smith (Malden, MA: Blackwell Publishers, 1992), 59.
6 Henri Lefebvre, *Writings on Cities*, ed. Eleonore Kofman and Elizabeth Lebas (Malden, MA: Blackwell Publishers, 1996),158.
7 Doug Saunders, *Arrival City: How the Largest Migration in History is Reshaping Our World* (New York: Pantheon, 2011).

unconscious, the disciplined and the transdisciplinary, everyday life and unending history."[4]

While Soja is influenced by Foucault, he also draws on the spatial trialectics of Henri Lefebvre, whose argument that space is a social construct, a complex social product that affects spatial practices and perceptions, has also influenced our thinking, especially with regard to the relationship between space and action: "Change life! Change society! These ideas lose completely their meaning without producing an appropriate space."[5] That imperative is informed by Lefebvre's notion of "the right to the city," calling for "a transformed and renewed access to urban life."[6]

Taken together, these precepts aptly describe both what Torre David is and what it does. But we would add to this the notion of the "arrival city," a typology identified, named, and described by Doug Saunders in his book of the same name.[7] He replaces the judgment-laden terms for squatter settlements—barrio, favela, slum, shantytown—with arrival city, a place of enormous energy and optimism, and argues that, far from seeking to tear them down and replace them with "urban renewal," we should nurture them by providing transportation, security, water and sewage treatment, and education.

These are, in effect, neither village nor city, but a third space that hybridizes the first two. Significantly for our research and projects, Saunders' typology relates explicitly to the immigrant enclave, meeting four essential criteria: It must act as an operable network, linking people locally and across great distances. It must provide an entryway for new arrivals, including affordable housing and employment. It presents opportunities for saving capital, making investments, accessing higher education, and participating directly in local politics. And finally, the arrival city includes a pathway for social mobility, leading out—or up—from the lower class toward sustainable membership in the urban core. It is our belief that the architectural typology that the Torre most represents—that of the growing house[8]—is the best suited to support such arrival cities. This is a physical and social design mechanism that can create and foster productive urban growth.

Among the considerable virtues of Soja's and Saunders' concepts is the implicit exclusion of the conventional utopia, the idealized "city on the hill" in which "[a]ll shall be well, and all shall be well, and all manner of things shall be well."[9] Instead, they propose an alternative utopia, based on reality, as described by Slavoj Zizek:

> We should reinvent utopia, but in what sense? There are two false meanings of utopia; one is the old notion of imagining an ideal society, which we know will never be realized. The other is the capitalist utopia in the sense of new perverse desires that you are not

8 U-TT developed and constructed a prototype design for incrementally developed residential buildings that we refer to as the "Growing House." The house provides the foundation for continual modifications and adaptations, even allowing for up to eight extra floors if residents' chose to construct vertically.

9 Julian of Norwich, 14th-century anchoress and Christian mystic; also quoted indirectly by T.S. Eliot in "Little Gidding."

only allowed but even solicited to realize. The true utopia is when the situation is so without issue, without a way to resolve it within the coordinates of the possible that out of the pure urge of survival you have to invent a new space. Utopia is not kind of a free imagination, utopia is a matter of inner-most urgency, you are forced to imagine this is the only way out, and this is the utopia we need today.[10]

From our point of view, utopia is not a place, specific and fixed in time and space; it is a methodology and a way of thinking and being. Utopianism, in that sense, has common ground with the notion of zero-defect manufacturing: it cannot be achieved, but if one behaves as though it were possible, it can be approached.[11]

Thus, we see Torre David as an arrival city, a laboratory for exploring and testing a utopian potential.

Barrio Petare, informal settlement.
Photo: U-TT/Erik-Jan Ouwerkerk

Torre David, informal vertical community. Photo: U-TT/Daniel Schwartz

23 de Enero, informal settlement occupying vacant land surrounding a modernist housing project.
Photo: U-TT/Bitter and Weber

10 Slavoj Zizek, *Zizek!,* directed by Astra Taylor [New York: Zeitgeist Films, 2006], DVD.
11 In a sense, it is akin to the principle of *imitatio Christi,* that living a Christ-like life brings one closer to creating an earthly paradise.

INTERVENING IN THE MEGA-CITY

Squatter settlements are not new, nor are they unique to Latin America. Nearly every mega-city in the world has its version: Caracas, Mexico City, Mumbai, Lagos, Johannesburg, Jakarta, Abuja, and Beijing. They differ in cultural conditions and expectations, in the geography that dictates their form and building materials, in the abundance or scarcity of basic resources such as water, and in the factors that drive people from rural areas to cities: poverty, famine, natural disaster, war. What they share is a population that grows with every driving impulse and that continues to grow exponentially.

Today, at least a billion people, perhaps even twice as many, live in slums on the fringes—literally, figuratively in high-rises such as Torre David, and in economic, social, and political terms—of the world's mega-cities.

Thus far, none of the large-scale reforms and interventions have resulted in a more workable, broadly applicable, and equitable city model than the one that has produced the asymmetries of the cities of the Global South. Approaches that involve large-scale, rapid change—the razing of slums, relocation of populations, infusions of money for major public works—have generally failed because a complex system such as a city can only absorb so much change at one time. They fail, too, from a reversal of the forest-and-trees perspective: governments, and the planners and designers they enlist, cannot see the trees—the individuals who occupy this vast informal world and the homes they have devised for themselves—for the forest, the "big picture" of the city grid, taken from a great height. The maps of these mega-cities typically do not even show evidence of squatter communities.

There are other obstacles to such urban renewal projects. Cities such as Caracas are already built up, even over-built. There are no sites left for greenfield projects and no money for grand schemes. Rather than erasing what already exists, we conceive of the "new" city as rooted in and arising from and with the old, as in the image on page 380/381. This essentially integrative vision makes connections, blurs distinctions, and effects a fundamental metamorphosis of the urban. It follows one of the classical principles of memory: we cannot willfully forget, but we can transform a memory by giving it new context and meaning.

We have already mentioned failed urban renewal projects such as many of the public housing developments in North America. In Caracas, where close to 60 percent of the population lives in the "informal" city, we have studied projects with far more sweeping impulses and consequences. Consider, for instance, the barrio of Petare, a more-than-60-year-old settlement on the eastern hills of Caracas with an estimated population in excess of one million living in just one square kilometer. With the oil boom of the 1970s, plans were formalized to build a six-lane highway connecting Caracas proper with the satellite cities to the east. A series of disputes, negotiations, and resolutions resulted in the transfer of ownership of the hills to the municipality, while the owners of the hillside land were compensated with a zoning ordinance for the flat land permitting construction of 14-story residential towers.

The highway is not the only thing that divides the barrio-dwellers from the residents of the private towers. The latter get no benefit from Venezuelan and World Bank funding designated for barrio upgrading; the former have seen no solutions to the problems of infrastructure or of their legal status. In the course of our research in Petare, we saw that inhabitants on both sides of the highway suffer from missing or badly maintained infrastructure, poor security, drug-related crime, and the lack of public spaces and recreation. Each side has fortified itself against the other, and everyone blames everyone else.

Barrio La Vega, one of Caracas' densest settlements, has also suffered from a version of the law of unintended consequences of official, if misplaced, attention and money. A key portion of the rehabilitation project for San Miguel, one sector of the barrio, was not only left incomplete, but has been partially dismantled for scrap. A new road and 48 resettlement housing units were only partially built.

Over the years, as we have explored the barrios in Latin American and around the world, consulted and collaborated with colleagues in various disciplines, and investigated the "informal city," we have taken a new and different approach, one that neither adheres to the conventional principles of urban renewal and planning nor treats the ad hoc, self-built environment as a romantic ideal. We abandoned that duality as we have rejected others that produce only adversarial stalemates. Instead, we deliberately employ micro-tactics, identifying small projects, working within communities and with their

Petare

All photos: U-TT/André Cypriano

leaders, trying and testing particular solutions to arrive at more general principles applicable to any informal city. Our approach, like that of the barrio-dwellers themselves, is bottom-up: reusing, adapting, and modifying the existing infrastructure, and retrofitting and stacking generatively. Ultimately, we are seeking to develop an industrially produced, interchangeable kit of parts that will serve as an essential quick-fix, an urban survival system for developing informal cities in urgent need of viable, affordable solutions.

Torre David is the first of our projects to take us from the hillside barrios, the informal fringes of the city, into the urban heart. But it is just the latest of the projects in which we have tested our interventions. These small- and medium-scale insertions into the existing landscape are intended to resolve specific problems of circulation, sanitation, housing, and recreation—flexible, quick-fix solutions to common urban ills. In 2005, for instance, we started construction on a vertical gymnasium on a 1,000-square-meter site in the densely populated Barrio La Cruz del Este. The project includes a basketball court, a running track, and a rooftop soccer field. Intended as a prototype for similar facilities in equally congested barrios, it serves an average of more than 15,000 visitors a month. In La Vega, with the support of the Ministry of the Environment, we began the installation of dry composting toilets, a response to the absence of a sewage system.[12] In Petare, we used "found space" under a highway overpass to insert a shelter for 30 homeless children, a playing field, and a woodwork shop.

Later, we designed a plan for a minimally invasive system of urban cable cars, as an alternative to roadways that would be impractical on the steep slopes of the barrios and would destroy existing housing. Working with the Doppelmayr/Garaventa Group and community residents we designed and completed the Caracas Metro Cable: a 2.1-kilometer cable car system, which has its beginning and end stations near public transportation, linking the barrio to the formal city. Three other stations are located along the crest of the hill.

La Vega

12 This project was a collaboration with Marjetica Portrč, Liyat Esakov, and the La Vega community.

Urban-Think Tank's Growing House prototype.

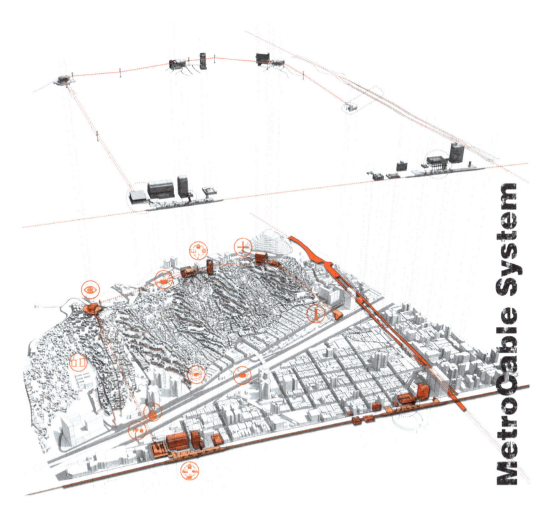

Urban-Think Tank's Caracas Metro Cable.

MetroCable System

Urban-Think Tank's Centro de Acçao Social por Música,
favela Paraisópolis, São Paulo.

Urban-Think Tank's Metro Cable, Barrio San Agustín,
Caracas.

One includes 40 units of housing, replacing dwellings demolished for the project; another includes athletic and recreational facilities. Launched in 2010, the system is able to transport up to 1,200 people per hour in each direction.

We continued to pursue the notion of a kit-of-parts, or toolbox, for meaningful interventions in the informal city with our students in the S.L.U.M. Lab (Sustainable Living Urban Model Laboratory) Studio at Columbia University's Graduate School of Architecture, Planning, and Preservation, and at the ETH Zürich Department of Architecture, as well as in our collaboration with São Paulo's Municipal Department of Housing (SEHAB). In the absence of potable water, for instance, we propose individual rainwater harvesting and the construction of common water tanks for storage. Shoddy and dangerous construction materials and methods could be replaced with a factory-built kit of components, whose assemblage is familiar to barrio residents and which accommodate small-scale development and dramatically enhance building quality. Now in the process of realization in São Paulo is the Centro de Acçao Social por Música, U-TT's urban remediation and civic infrastructure hub. [13]

Projects such as these are, however, only small pieces of a larger picture and a longer-term goal that we have set for Urban-Think Tank. We have deliberately shifted our attention from the formal city of master plans, commissions, and the traditional client-architect relationship, to the informal city of slums, with millions of impoverished "clients," isolated from global capital, and sometimes occupying land illegally. Coming from Caracas we have sought a new set of design tools specifically tailored to the city. But because we believe that Caracas as a manifestation is everywhere, the global urban norm rather than the exception, we also seek solutions whose adaptability, sustainability, and basis in the fundamental principles of an equitable quality of life make them suitable for near-universal application. In so doing, and through our discourse with colleagues around the world, we hope to help shift the focus of contemporary architectural practice away from its preoccupation with form, toward a marriage of design with social impact.

13 This project has received both the 2011 Gold (Latin America) Holcim Award, and the 2012 Silver (Global) Holcim Award, for its achievement in sustainable Construction.

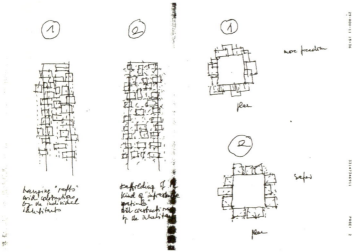

During the course of our research over the past two years we continually returned to the ideas of Yona Friedman, seeking insight and inspiration through personal correspondence and his published work.

In May 2012, Yona welcomed U-TT into his home in Paris to discuss Torre David. Impressed by stories of the residents' ingenuity, he sketched possible futures for the Tower. These are his drawings.

A CHALLENGE TO THE ARCHITECTURAL PROFESSION

One of the biggest problems in cities today is the failure of decision-makers to identify and contribute actively to a larger vision. Indeed, the absence of vision—both in the sense of foresightedness and of truly seeing one's surroundings—is part of a general abdication of responsibility: the inhabitants of large cities and those they elect both defer judgment and decisions to "experts," on the assumption that the latter know best. To the contrary, we have found that projects conceived, promulgated, designed, and realized by the expert architects and planners all too often are abject failures, because they are founded in formal 19th- and 20th-century models and urban vocabularies. The urban and architectural theories and ideologies emerging from the university and from "signature" architects fail precisely where they should be most intensely focused: on the city as a place for equal opportunities, urban culture, and policies in the service and well-being of the citizens. The missing thread in the discussions of form and style and urban development is accountability to those whose lives are directly affected.

Far from being irrelevant to the development of the informal city, architects are much needed. But they will have to be a different kind of architect, open to different ways of thinking both about design and about the role and responsibilities of the profession in the social, economic, and political arenas. They will need to be actively and continually engaged with professionals in other disciplines, not in theoretical discussions of utopian ideals, but in the creation and realization of viable, innovative interventions. And we believe that our profession, architecture, in particular needs a profoundly different concept of "innovation," one that has almost nothing to do with the latest design "-ism" and everything to do with *purpose.*

To those ends, we propose to challenge the conventions of architectural training and practice:

Question everything you think you know—not because everything you have learned is irrelevant, but because its relevance has changed. Question everything you see—by asking not "what is it?" but "why is it?" The "what" questions lead us backward, trying to fit what we see into what we already assume. "Why" questions go to the heart of the needs, desires, and impulses of those we serve. Ask questions of people—not programmatic questions, but personal ones, especially those concerning their relationship with place and space.

Assume scarcity, especially of financial and natural resources. Use it to provoke innovation and excellence. Mies was right: less *is* more, but not in the way he meant it. Less is simply a fact of life for more and more people. Make recycling the first choice, not a fall-back position or merely a clever design feature. Consider the innovative possibilities of recycling unused or poorly used land. Test new materials and methods. Be bold. Take chances.

Don't wait for local policies and laws to dictate sustainable strategies and regulations—act as though sustainability were the key design imperative. Think broadly about what sustainability really means in the context of the lives your work affects.

Ask big questions. If the city—the building, the home, the street grid, the transportation system—as we know it did not exist, what would we invent? Act as though we really could begin again anew, so as to move closer to what we should have.

Do not assume that design innovation—indeed, architectural excellence—as taught in and promulgated by the academy and real-world practice in the informal city or rural areas are mutually exclusive. To the contrary, they can be mutually enriching, when they overlap and bring the strength of each into the realm of the other. Schools of architecture and architectural practices can produce creative, workable, cost-effective designs and prototypes for real-world application.

So, too, can the private sector. Partner with companies that value research, development, and innovation; provide them with living laboratories in which to rest and refine their products. Teach them what you know; learn from them what they know.

Pursuing fairness and equity does not mean abandoning design vision. Indeed, accomplishing those ends requires the capacity to envision that which does not yet exist. Aesthetics and ethics—or, in other words, the beautiful and the useful—are not mutually exclusive.

Nor should integration come at the cost of variety. The collective good need not sacrifice individualism. Create guidelines, principles, toolkits; provide an infrastructure. Then help put these to use by enabling individual, local, and regional variations.

Eschew the binary; embrace multiplicity. Build bridges, not walls, networks, not moats. It is the responsibility of the architect to identify common ground and then to build upon it.

Teach everyone. Learn from everyone. Share knowledge, expertise, and advice, by introducing developers and residents to principles of sound construction techniques, methods of recycling, properties of different materials, relationships between form and function, so that interventions have real and lasting value in the community.

Cross disciplinary boundaries to collaborate with those in other fields. The role of the architect is to integrate disparate knowledge into a meaningful, useful tool for change.

Let go of architectural formalism, of "purity" of design as the goal and honors as the reward. Re-engage the discipline and its practice with the essential task of defining and shaping the future of the city. Architects can no longer take an amoral position with regard to their creations if they wish to remain relevant and useful.

Adages tend to become clichés when they are true: make "think globally, act locally" a foundational principle of architectural practice. Innovations and best practices are everywhere—but they must be revisited and revised to suit the particular place and culture.

Whether the impetus is noble or base, reforms enacted and imposed from the top down—by governments, international agencies, and experts—have not succeeded completely or in the long-term. Either they fail to account for the realities of the lives they intend to better; or they are undermined by inadequate or absent maintenance and security; or both. Any intervention in the informal city takes place within a complex process of democratization: the inhabitants are there to judge the results by the extent to which the solutions are practical and have the capacity to improve living conditions for all those affected. Absent consultation with and the participation of those immediately affected, it is impossible to understand fully the real conditions in which they live, their needs and aspirations, and their perspective. As Francisco Perez, a La Vega community leader, said when we were preparing *Informal City: Caracas Case*,[14] "What you call a barrio I call my home."

To date, efforts to "deal with" slums, wherever they appear, have focused on their eradication, with the objective of creating a slum-free world. Rather than seeing slums as tumors on the civic body, we conceive them as potentially vital, vibrant laboratories, from whose successes we can learn and whose failures we can seek to mitigate. They hold the potential for extraordinary design innovation and exceptional architectural achievement.

The informal expands, reproduces, and generates new structures and new alternatives to the traditional urban grid, in a process of incremental development. It is the way of the urban future, one that is antithetical to notions of completeness and finality. It is what we found in Torre David. It is thus also antithetical to that for which we architects were trained and to our expectations for practice and for reward. But architects and their professional colleagues must awaken to the realization that we serve all humanity, regardless of location or means—and we serve at the pleasure of those whom our work affects. Let us seek to be remembered not only for the brick-and-mortar of our accomplishments, but for their capacity to contribute meaningfully to society.

It is time for professionals—urban planners, social activists, engineers, and most especially architects—to confront the realities of the future by helping to develop the urban fabric from the ground up; to interact forcefully but productively with politicians, policy-makers, and community groups; to enlist the private sector in developing and deploying innovations; and to participate collectively in the creation of more equitable, workable, and sustainable cities.

14 Alfredo Brillembourg, Kristin Feireiss, and Hubert Klumpner, eds., *Informal City: Caracas Case* (New York: Prestel Publishing, 2005).

Section perspective: Torre David as it stands today.

Torre David with potential retrofits.

Re-imagining the new city as rooted in and growing
from the old.

"Intelligence starts with improvisation."

—Yona Friedman

AFTERWORD:
URBANIZATION AS AN OPEN PROCESS

Christian Schmid

A 45-story commercial high-rise where some three thousand people live with-out air conditioning, without elevators, and with minimal infrastructure, made habitable only through improvisation—this is undoubtedly one of the most extreme contemporary examples of the appropriation of urban space. At first glance, the scenario may seem absurd. Yet, as this book shows, it is a very real and highly impressive example of social reality in today's urban environment. The apparent strangeness of this case study offers a screen onto which all manner of ideas can be projected. It calls into question many things that are usually taken for granted and undermines the concept of planned and organized urban development. In that respect, it has implications far beyond this specific case and raises some fundamental issues about urbanization and architecture.

HIGH-RISE

One of the first things we learn from this example is about the nature of the high-rise itself: we realize that a high-rise is more than just a tall building. It is a complex, socio-technical system with its own distinctive reality. When re-duced to a mere skeleton, it is barely habitable. While this fact, demonstrated *in vivo* by Torre David, may be obvious to architects, it is something that most city-dwellers rarely even consider. There is, for instance, the air-conditioning system without which such a building, fully enclosed by its façade, would be uninhabitable. For fresh air and cooling, the people who live in Torre David have broken through parts of the façade—solving ventilation problems but exposing themselves to unpredictable climate conditions. And then there are electricity, water, and sewage disposal, not to mention the transport system of elevators without which a building such as this, with its own spatiotemporal logistics, cannot function normally.

AN EXPERIMENT

This building was originally intended as an office and commercial complex—not as a barrio. It is a failed project in the heart of the city, abruptly abandoned in an unfinished and practically unusable state owing to the vagaries of his-toric developments—and now it is being used in a way that was never envis-aged. The word "high-rise" no longer describes the building; it has become

I have never been to Caracas, so I have no personal firsthand experience of Torre David. The thoughts expressed here are based on many conversations with Alfredo Brillembourg and Hubert Klumpner, on the large quantity of material gathered in this book, and on my own research and experience in Zurich, Paris, Havana, and other cities.

something for which we have no adequate term. The limitations and the potential of a high-rise have been explored here in radical ways and at the same time they have been deconstructed—not as an artistic project, but in real life. It is a very special kind of social experiment with an uncertain outcome.

SOCIAL LIFE

"What the hell is going on here?" is one of the classic questions posed by sociologists exploring an unknown social situation in their fieldwork. Faced with the Torre David experiment, the architects who have written this book have become sociologists, examining reality and discovering the sociological motive at the heart of architecture. Through interviews and participatory observation, they provide us with a precise insight into social actions and processes. The role of social life is brought to the fore: we discover how societal models are developed, how forms of cooperation and cohabitation evolve, and how new rules emerge and become established. We also learn about the social implications of the built environment and the possibilities of using architectural structures in ways for which they were not originally intended.

SQUAT

"This tower is a squat" may sound like a clear-cut statement. But what exactly is a squat? It can take many different forms with many different implications. Squatting may be a political act, a means of appropriating urban spaces, a way of finding a place to live, through necessity or even sheer desperation. As anyone who has ever considered the issue knows, squats always have a history, a social structure and, for the most part, an element of political organization. They are rarely a spontaneous occurrence. Similarly, the squatters of Torre David did not move into the building in a purely spontaneous act—there is a lengthy backstory, which is outlined in detail in this book.

SELF-ORGANIZATION

Squatters invariably have to find solutions to specific problems. Only rarely do they have a situation where they can simply move in to comfortable, fit-for-use premises. For the most part, a great deal of commitment, hard work, and creative energy are required in order to make the place habitable. Because of this, squatters develop specific forms of self-organization with their own social structures and rules to shape their community and cope with everyday life. Torre David is unusual in this respect, too, as it requires an even higher degree of self-organization, not only because of its size, but also because of the particular circumstances of the building.

APPROPRIATING THE CITY

Torre David is an extreme example of appropriating and adapting unfinished or diverted structures. It is, in many respects, to be regarded not so much as an individual building, but rather as part of a city. It might be described as a part of the urban fabric that has been tipped into the vertical, creating some added problems, admittedly, but nevertheless fundamentally the same as any other part of the urban fabric. Every city, after all, is based on a built environment in which there is a relatively rigid and inert structure that determines the rhythm of daily life and cannot be altered without enormous effort. And yet, with a little imagination and intelligence, even these structures can be used in different ways, as Torre David so clearly illustrates.

INFORMALITY

The process of urbanization occurring outside the bounds of legally defined structures and beyond the scope of established rules of planning, urban design, and architectural procedures, is often described as informal. What was originally regarded as a merely temporary aberration or deviation from the norm has since become so widespread in so many cities that it no longer appears to be the exception. Informality stands for flexibility and grey areas, but also for hazardous situations. Torre David, for instance, has many areas that should not be used because they are too precarious—exposed stairways without railings, passages with large gaps in the floor, and other such dangers. In this respect, formality is a matter of protecting the inhabitants; where it is lacking there may well be greater freedom—but there are also greater insecurity and risk. However, there are very different types of informality and, in one way or another, some kind of formality is always involved in the form of regulations, norms, and procedures. The authors of this book demonstrate that through hierarchical leadership and management, Torre David develops towards order and formality, not away from it.

URBAN SITUATIONS

In short, the starting point here is an unplanned and unforeseen situation. As in many other cases, this reflects the essential qualities of urban life: unpredictability, open-ended development, the possibility of surprising encounters and coincidences. When cities lose that openness and are developed and built without any input from the inhabitants themselves, a very crucial quality is lacking. In this respect, Torre David also represents the possibilities and potential of the unfinished and challenges us to create open, flexible structures.

URBANIZATION AS A PROCESS OF INNOVATION

This brings us to the question of urbanization itself. It is invariably a process of exploration, shaped as much by existing structures as it is by chance and sudden events. The city is a place in constant flux. And so, urban development is, by definition, a process that requires constant innovation and inventiveness. Situations arise that call for new solutions, sometimes resulting in completely different and unexpected qualities. Errors and dead ends are as much a part of that as serendipitous breakthroughs and success stories. That makes the city an experimental field upon which the rich diversity of society can flourish.

THE LIMITS OF ARCHITECTURE

Many current urban situations are just as unusual as Torre David. How should we approach them? Should they be demolished and replaced with new buildings, thereby destroying the social structures that have developed organically? Or should they be improved and extended in ways that integrate their informal structures into the existing system and tame the anarchy? Given these alternatives, we have to ask ourselves what role the urban specialists play at all in today's urban development. Countless examples in urban spaces fundamentally question the role of architects, urban developers, and planners. These questions should trigger debate: what can and should architects and town planners do? What role do professionals and academics play in these processes? How can they promote the creation of a different, more just society?

OPEN DEVELOPMENT

The example of Torre David is one of many narratives from the familiar, and unfamiliar, history of urbanization. What can we learn from it? There are already enough texts offering us lessons for the future. This is a different story—one with an open end that emerges from a continually advancing, real-world present. Many lessons can be learned from it. We may not be able to deduce any clear strategies from such an example, but we can let it inspire us. The city is a work in progress. We should keep our minds open to new alternatives and even unexpected routes of development.

APPENDIX

BIBLIOGRAPHY

Albornoz, Maye. "El Sambil es otra 'torre de David.'" *El Universal* (Caracas). May 9, 2011. http://www.eluniversal.com/2011/05/09/el-sambil-es-otra-torre-de-david.shtml.

Aquacraft, Inc. "Embedded Energy in Water: Study 3. End-Use Water Demand Profile – Final Research Plan." California Institute for Energy and Environment. January 7, 2009. Accessed May 2, 2012. http://uc-ciee.org/downloads/Eeiswtudy3.pdf.

Armas H., Mayela. "Emergency Law Paves the Way for Seizure of Lands and Storehouses." Translated by Gerardo Cárdenas. *El Universal* (Caracas). February 1, 2011. http://www.eluniversal.com/2011/02/01/en_eco_esp_emergency-law-paves_01A5089293.shtml.

———. "Venezuelan Antitrust Bill Establishes More Ways to Expropriate." Translated by Karen Daza. *El Universal* (Caracas). May 23, 2012. http://www.eluniversal.com/economia/120523/venezuelan-antitrust-bill-establishes-more-ways-to-expropriate.

Asamblea Nacional Constituyente, Caracas, 1999. "Constitution of the Bolivarian Republic of Venezuela." Caracas: Ministerio de Comunicación e Información, 2006. http://www.analitica.com/bitblioteca/venezuela/constitucion_ingles.pdf.

Associated Press. "Venezuelan Flood Victims Can Stay at Presidential Palace, Says Hugo Chávez." *The Guardian.* December 2, 2010. http://www.guardian.co.uk/world/2010/dec/02/venezuela-flood-victims-hugo-chavez.

Brillembourg, David, Jr. Interviewed by Ilana Millner and Daniel Schwartz. Caracas/Zurich. July 2, 2012.

Brooke, James. "International Report; Latin America Pursues Recovery on 2 Fronts." *New York Times.* August 28, 1989. http://www.nytimes.com/1989/08/28/business/international-report-latin-america-pursues-recovery-on-2-fronts.html.

Brophy, Vivienne, Crea O'Dowd, Rachel Bannon, John Goulding, and J. Owen Lewis. "Sustainable Urban Design." *Energie.* Dublin: European Commission, 2000. Accessed March 5, 2012. http://www.scribd.com/doc/19231594/Architecture-Sustainable-Urban-Design.

Buxton, Julia. "Economic Policy and the Rise of Hugo Chávez." In *Venezuelan Politics in the Chávez Era,* edited by Steve Ellner and Daniel Hellinger, 113–30. Boulder, CO: Lynne Rienner Publishers, Inc. 2003.

"Caracas is the World's Third Most Violent Sub-National Jurisdiction." *El Universal* (Caracas). April 27, 2012. http://www.eluniversal.com/nacional-y-politica/120427/caracas-is-the-worlds-third-most-violent-sub-national-jurisdiction.

Carroll, Rory. "Chávez Tackles Housing Crisis by Urging Poor to Squat Wealthy Parts of Caracas." *The Guardian.* January 26, 2011. http://www.guardian.co.uk/world/2011/jan/26/venezuela-chavez-housing-crisis-squats-caracas.

Castro, Maolis. "Libertador es territorio de invasiones." *El Nacional* (Caracas). March 5, 2012.

"Chaos in Caracas." *The Economist.* April 10, 1997. http://www.economist.com/node/1044426.

"Chávez Raises Oil Production in Venezuela." *New York Times.* January 29, 2003. http://www.nytimes.com/2003/01/29/international/americas/29VENE.html.

"Chávez retoma paralización del Sambil La Candelaria." *El Universal* (Caracas). June 11, 2009. http://www.eluniversal.com/2009/06/11/ccs_ava_chavez-retoma-parali_11A2383971.shtml.

Consorcio Energético Corpoema. "Formulación de un plan de desarrollo paralas Fuentes no convencionales de energiía en Colombia (PFDNCE)." Bogotá: Unidad de Planeación Minero Energética UPME, December 30, 2010. Accessed May 13, 2012. http://www.corpoema.com/pdf/Vol%203%20Tecnologia%20y%20Costos%20FNCE.pdf.

Cooperativa de Vivienda Caciques de Venezuela. "Diseño Nueva Fachada." *Historias de la Torre Confinanzas.* June 27, 2011. Accessed May 2, 2012. http://torreconfinanza.blogspot.ch/2011/06/diseno-nueva-fachada.html.

Corpoelec Empresa Eléctrica Socialista. "Profesionales debaten interrupciones eléctricas." *Corpolec Informa* 1, (August 5, 2011): 11. http://www.corpoelec.gob.ve/corpoelec-informa.

"Coup and Counter-Coup." *The Economist.* April 16, 2002. http://www.economist.com/node/1086376.

Cruz Salazar, Beatriz. "Miedo se Palpa Cerca de la Torre." *El Universal* (Caracas). September 8, 2008. http://www.eluniversal.com/2008/09/08/ccs_art_miedo-se-palpa-cerca_1028602.shtml.

"The Devil's Excrement." *The Economist,* May 22, 2003. http://www.economist.com/node/1795921.

Ehsan, M. M., Enaiyat Ghani Ovy, Kazy Fayeen Shariar, and S.M. Ferdous. "A Novel Approach of Electrification of the High Rise Buildings at Dhaka City During Load Shedding Hours." *International Journal of Renewable Energy Research* 2, no. 4 (2012): 123–30. http://ijrer.net/index.php/ijrer/article/view/140/pdf.

Ellner, Steve. "Introduction: The Search for Explanations." In *Venezuelan Politics in the Chávez Era,* edited by Steve Ellner and Daniel Hellinger, 7–26. Boulder, CO: Lynne Rienner Publishers, Inc. 2003.

———. "The Contrasting Variants of the Populism of Hugo Chávez and Alberto Fujimori." *Journal of Latin American Studies* 35, no. 1 (February 2003): 139–62. http://www.jstor.org/stable/387558.

European Commission. "Country Energy Information: Venezuela." September 2006. Accessed March 8, 2012. http://www.energyrecipes.org/reports/genericData/Latin%20America/061129%20RECIPES%20country%20info%20Venezuela.pdf.

European Environment Agency (EEA). "Final Energy Consumption by Sector (CSI 027/ENER 016)." Copenhagen: European Environment Agency (EEA), March 29, 2012. Last modified April 30, 2012. Accessed May 2, 2012. http://www.eea.europa.eu/data-and-maps/indicators/final-energy-consumption-by-sector-2/final-energy-consumption-by-sector-7.

Facultad de Ciencias, Universidad Nacional de Colombia. "Determinación del consume final de energía en los sectores residencial urbano y commercial y determinación de consumes para equipos domesticos de energiía eléctrica y gas." Paper presented to Unidad de Planeación Minero Energética UPME. Bogotá: June 11, 2006. http://www.siel.gov.co/siel/documentos/documentacion/Demanda/Residencial/Consumo_Final_Energia.swf.

"Familias de la Torre Confinanzas protestan en el Ministerio del Interior." *El Universal* (Caracas). April 11, 2012. http://playball.eluniversal.com/caracas/120411/familias-de-la-torre-confinanzas-protestan-en-el-ministerio-del-interi.

Fondo de Garantía de Depósitos y Protección Bancaria (FOGADE). "Objetivo." Gobierno Bolivariano de Venezuela. Accessed July 27, 2012. http://fogade.gob.ve/Objetivos/Objetivos.htm.

Forero, Juan. "Venezuela Land Reform Looks to Seize Idle Farmland." *New York Times.* January 30, 2005. http://query.nytimes.com/gst/fullpage.html?res=9400EFDD153BF933A05752C0A9639C8B63&pagewanted=all.

Freer, Jim. "Prime Venezuelan Land Available Through Auction." *South Florida Business Journal.* June 25, 2001. http://www.bizjournals.com/southflorida/stories/2001/06/25/story7.html?page=all.

Fuenmayor, Jésus. "The Tower of David." *Domus.* April 28, 2011. http://www.domusweb.it/en/architecture/the-tower-of-david/.

"Fundacomunal asegura que los terrenos son baldíos." *El Universal* (Caracas). January 22, 2011. http://www.eluniversal.com/2011/01/22/ccs_ava_fundacomunal-asegura_22A5026371.shtml.

Gómez, Enrique, and Julio Rey. Interviewed by Rafael Machado and Mathieu Quillici. Caracas. February 15, 2012.

González, Felipe, and Carlos Crespo. "TSJ argumentó que invasiones ya no son delito en Venezuela." *El Tiempo.* December 12, 2011. http://eltiempo.com.ve/venezuela/tribunales/tsj-argumento-que-invasiones-ya-no-son-delito-en-venezuela/39480.

González Saavedra, Carlos. "El Musmon Vuelve A La Carga: Confianza En Las Alturas." *Inmuebles* (Caracas). September 30, 1992.

Haggerty, Richard A., and Howard I. Blutstein. *Venezuela: A Country Study.* Edited by Richard A. Haggerty and Howard I. Blutstein. Washington, DC: GPO for the Library of Congress. 1990. http://countrystudies.us/venezuela/.

Hall, Fred, and Roger Greeno. *Building Services Handbook: Incorporating Current Building and Construction Regulations.* 5th edition. New York: Elseiver Science, 2009.

Hellinger, Daniel. "Political Overview: The Breakdown of Puntofijismo and the Rise of Chavismo." In *Venezuelan Politics in the Chávez Era,* edited by Steve Ellner and Daniel Hellinger, 27–54. Boulder, CO: Lynne Rienner Publishers, Inc. 2003.

The Heritage Foundation. "2012 Index of Economic Freedom." Accessed April 25, 2012. www.heritage.org/index/country/venezuela.

Hernández Dávila, Gerardo. "La Torre de David." *El Universal* (Caracas). September 1, 2007. http://www.eluniversal.com/2007/09/01/opi_36199_art_la-torre-de-david_01A975957.shtml.

Hughes, Tim. "Lesson number 1. In an Oklahoma Wind Power Tutorial Series." Lecture presented at Oklahoma State University, Stillwater, OK, April 2, 2000. Accessed April 10, 2012. http://www.ocgi.okstate.edu/owpi/EducOutreach/Library/Lesson1_windenergycalc.pdf.

Inter-American Development Bank (IDB). "Executive Summary: Room for Development." 2012. http://idbdocs.iadb.org/.

———. "Home Ownership Unaffordable for Many in Latin America and the Caribbean, IDB Study Finds." May 14, 2012. http://www.iadb.org/.

International Energy Agency (IEA). "Worldwide Trends in Energy Use and Efficiency." Paris: 2008. http://www.iea.org/papers/2008/indicators_2008.pdf.

Jancovici, Jean-Marc. "A Tool for Companies and Office Activities: The 'Carbon Inventory' of ADEME." Manicore. May 2004. Accessed April 25, 2012. http://www.manicore.com/anglais/missions_a/carbon_inventory.html.

Jarzombek, Mark. "Sustainability in Architecture: Between Fuzzy Systems and Wicked Problems." *Blueprints* 11, no. 1 (Winter 2003): 7–9. http://web.mit.edu/mmj4/www/downloads/blueprints21_1.pdf.

Joint Research Centre, European Commission.
"Performance of Grid-connected PV: help, calculation methodology." Accessed April 18, 2012. http://re.jrc.ec.europa.eu/pvgis/apps3/pvest.php.

Kraul, Chris. "Venezuela Polarized Over Chavez's Land Policy." *Los Angeles Times.* April 7, 2011. http://articles.latimes.com/print/2011/apr/07/world/la-fg-venezuela-squatters-20110408.

Land, Peter. Interviewed by Daniel Schwartz. May 24, 2012.

Lerch Bates. "Vertical Transportation: Design Guidelines and Technology." Lecture presented at AIA (American Institute of Architects) Los Angeles, Los Angeles, CA, July 1, 2009. Accessed May 5, 2012. http://www.aialaarchive.org/events/assets_images/2009MobiusLA/presentations/Vertical_Transport_Elevator_Design.pdf.

Lombardi, John V. "Prologue: Venezuela's Permanent Dilemma." In *Venezuelan Politics in the Chávez Era,* edited by Steve Ellner and Daniel Hellinger, 1–6. Boulder: Lynne Rienner Publishers, Inc. 2003.

Long, Seth. "Land Reform in Venezuela." *Counter Punch.* February 26–28, 2005. http://www.counterpunch.org/2005/02/26/land-reform-in-venezuela/.

López Maya, Margarita. "Hugo Chávez Frías: His Movement and His Presidency." In *Venezuelan Politics in the Chávez Era,* edited by Steve Ellner and Daniel Hellinger, 73–91. Boulder, CO: Lynne Rienner Publishers, Inc. 2003.

———. "The Venezuelan *Caracazo* of 1989: Popular Protest and Institutional Weakness." *Journal of Latin American Studies* 35, no. 1 (Feb. 2003): 117–37. http://www.jstor.org/stable/3875580.

Lown, Zachary. "The Conflict Between State-led Revolution and Popular Militancy in Venezuela." *venezuelanalysis.com.* Sept. 2, 2009. http://venezuelanalysis.com/analysis/4763.

Márquez, Patricia. "The Hugo Chávez Phenomenon: What Do 'the People' Think?" In *Venezuelan Politics in the Chávez Era,* edited by Steve Ellner and Daniel Hellinger, 197–213. Boulder, CO: Lynne Rienner Publishers, Inc. 2003.

Meneses, Delia. "Convivencia se hace tensa en predios de Sambil Candelaria." *El Universal* (Caracas). January 1, 2012. http://www.eluniversal.com/caracas/120112/convivencia-se-hace-tensa-en-predios-de-sambil-candelaria.

———. "Un barrio en Sambil Candelaria." *El Universal* (Caracas). September 23, 2011. http://www.eluniversal.com/2011/09/23/un-barrio-en-sambil-candelaria.shtml.

Ministerio del Poder Popular para la Energía Electrica (MPPEE). "Hacer Uso Eficiente y Racional de Energía es Un Deber." Caracas: Gobierno Bolivariano de Venezuela, 2011. Accessed April 14, 2012. http://www.mppee.gob.ve/uploads/65/c0/65c07baf7a2a168b0b169e748ae979d1/ENCARTE-WEB-Resolucion.pdf.

———. "Medidas para el Ahorro Energetico: Rueda de Prensa." Caracas: Gobierno Bolivariano de Venezuela, June 13, 2011. Accessed April 14, 2012. http://www.mppee.gob.ve/uploads/a4/5a/a45ae10b86e2152d8bcf604d4952ef40/medidas_electricasweb20110615-0900.pdf.

Motorwave. "Product Description." 2011. Accessed May 2, 2012. http://www.motorwavegroup.com/new/motorwind/product.html.

Naím, Moisés. "The Devil's Excrement." *Foreign Policy.* September/October 2009. http://www.foreignpolicy.com/articles/2009/08/17/the_devil_s_excrement.

National Meteorological Library and Archive. "Fact Sheet 6 – The Beaufort Scale." London: Met Office, 2010. Accessed April 17, 2012. http://www.metoffice.gov.uk/media/pdf/4/4/Fact_Sheet_No._6_-_Beaufort_Scale.pdf.

Nielsen, Anders, and Jens Nøorgaard. "Water Supply in Tall Buildings: Roof Tanks vs. Pressurized Systems." Grundfos. 2010. Accessed April 15, 2012. http://www.scribd.com/doc/90499444/Roof-Tank-Whitepaper.

Odyssee. "Consumption per Dwelling." *Energy Efficiency Indicators in Europe.* Accessed July 5, 2012. *http://www.odyssee-indicators.org/online-indicators/.*

Organisation for Economic Co-operation and Development (OECD). *Energy Balances of OECD Countries 2010.* International Energy Agency (IEA). 2010.

Parliamentary Office of Science and Technology. "Carbon Footprint of Electricity Generation." No. 268. London: October 2006. Accessed May 2, 2012. http://www.parliament.uk/documents/post/postpn268.pdf.

Pearson, Tamara. "New Venezuelan Law Turns Unused Urban Land Into Public Land." *venezuelanalysis.com.* August 16, 2009. http://venezuelanalysis.com/news/4726.

Peters, Richard, Pratap Mehta, and John Haddon. "Lift Passenger Traffic Patterns: Applications, Current Knowledge and Measurement." Paper presented at The International Congress on Vertical Transportation Technologies, Barcelona, 1996. Accessed June 12, 2012. http://www.peters-research.com/index.php?option=com_content&view=article&id=57%3Alift-passenger-traffic-patterns-applications-current-knowledge-and-measurement&catid=3%3Apapers&Itemid=1.

Patterson, Terry. *Illustrated 2009 Building Code Handbook.* New York: McGraw-Hill Professional, 2009.

Petroleos de Venezuela S.A. "Proyecto Bombona Communal: del pueblo para el pueblo." Accessed June 12, 2012. http://www.pdvsa.com/index.php?tpl= interface.sp/design/readmenu.tpl.html&newsid_obj_ id=4595&newsid_temas=54.

"Police Force Raids Confinanzas Tower Based on Phone Calls Triangulation." *El Universal* (Caracas). April 9, 2012. http://www.eluniversal.com/nacional-y-politica/120409/police-force-raids-confinanzas-tower-based-on-phone-calls-triangulatio.

Powell, Bruce A. "An Alternate Approach to Traffic Analysis for Residential Buildings." Paper presented at The International Congress on Vertical Transportation Technologies, Thessaloniki, 2008. http://www.peters-research.com/index.php?option= com_content&view=article&id=105%3Aan-alternate-approach-to-traffic-analysis-for-residential-buildings &catid=3%3Apapers&Itemid=1.

Ramírez Miranda, Deivis. "Torre de David sospechosa de secuestro." *El Universal* (Caracas). April 10, 2012. http://www.eluniversal.com/sucesos/120410/torre-de-david-sospechosa-de-secuestro.

Rifkin, Jeremy. *The Third Industrial Revolution: How Lateral Power is Transforming Energy, the Economy, and the World.* New York: Palgrave Macmillan, 2011.

Rodríguez, Rafael. "Denuncian 20 intentos invasiones en Chacao." *El Universal* (Caracas). January 22, 2011. http://www.eluniversal.com/2011/01/22/ccs_ava_ denuncian-20-intento_22A5025171.shtml.

———. "Sambil La Candelaria pasará a ser refugio para damnificados." *El Universal* (Caracas). December 2, 2010. http://www.eluniversal.com/2010/12/02/pol_ava_ sambil-la-candelaria_02A4807773.shtml.

Rohter, Larry. "A Divided Venezuela Votes on a New Charter Today." *New York Times.* December 15, 1999. http://www.nytimes.com/1999/12/15/ world/a-divided-venezuela-votes-on-new-charter-today. html?pagewanted=all&src=pm.

———. "Months Later, Mud Victims in Venezuela Still Lack Aid." *New York Times.* April 16, 2000. http://www.nytimes.com/2000/04/16/world/months-later-mud-victims-in-venezuela-still-lack-aid.html.

———. "Venezuelan Leader Pushes for New Charter, but Is It Reformist Tool or a Power Grab?" *New York Times.* July 25, 1999. http://www.nytimes.com/1999/07/25/ world/venezuelan-leader-pushes-for-new-charter-but-it-reformist-tool-power-grab.html?pagewanted= all&src=pm.

Romero, Simon. "Chávez Keeping His Promise to Redistribute Land." *New York Times.* May 16, 2007. http://www.nytimes.com/2007/05/17/world/americas/ 17iht-17venezuela.5749093.html?pagewanted=all.

———. "Legislature Grants Chávez Broad New Powers to Shape Venezuela." *New York Times.* February 1, 2007. http://select.nytimes.com/gst/abstract.html?res=F2061 5FB3E5B0C728CDDAB0894DF404482.

Romleu, Isabelle, Weitzenfeld W., and Finkelman, J. "Urban Air Pollution in Latin America and the Caribbean." *Journal of the Air and Waste Management Association* 41, no. 9 (1991): 1166–1171.

Ruskin, John. *The Seven Lamps of Architecture.* London: Smith, Elder, and co., 1849.

Siikonen, Marja-Liisa. "On Traffic Planning Methodology." Paper presented at The International Congress on Vertical Transportation Technologies, Berlin, 2000. Accessed April 17, 2012. http://www.kone.com/countries/ sitecollectiondocuments/mp/elevcon2000_traffic_ planning.pdf.

Staan, Jeffrey E. "Transportation and Urbanization in Caracas, 1891–1936." *Journal of Interamerican Studies and World Affairs* 17, no. 1 (Feb. 1975): 82–100. http://www.jstor.org/stable/174789.

Starr, Alexandra. "Caracas: Living Large on Oil." *The American Scholar.* Spring 2007. http://theamericanscholar.org/letter-from-caracas/.

The Swiss Wind Power Data Website. "The Weibull Calculator." Accessed April 10, 2012. http://www.wind-data.ch/tools/weibull.php.

The Swiss Wind Power Data Website. "Wind Profile Calculator." Accessed April 10, 2012. http://www.winddata.ch/tools/profile.php?h=10&v= 3.5&z0=0.1&abfrage=Refresh.

Tarver, H. Michael, and Julia C. Frederick. *The History of Venezuela.* Westport, CT: Greenwood Press, 2005.

Thompson, Ginger. "Venezuela's Oil Chief Says He Will Make Big Changes." *New York Times.* December 25, 2002. http://www.nytimes.com/2002/12/25/world/ venezuela-s-oil-chief-says-he-will-make-big-changes. html?pagewanted=all&src=pm.

UN-HABITAT (United Nations Human Settlements Programme). "Affordable Land and Housing in Latin America and the Caribbean." 2011. www.unhabitat.org.

United Nations Environment Programme. "Sustainable Building and Construction: Facts and Figures." *Industry and Environment* 26, no. 2–3 (April–September 2003). http://www.uneptie.org/ media/review/vol26no2-3/005-098.pdf.

United Nations General Assembly. "Resolution 60/1. 2005 World Summit Outcome." New York: United Nations, October 24, 2005. http://data.unaids.org/Topics/UniversalAccess/worldsummitoutcome_resolution_24oct2005_en.pdf.

U.S. Department of Energy. EnergyPlus Energy Simulation Software: Weather Data Venezuela. Accessed May 18, 2012. http://apps1.eere.energy.gov/buildings/energyplus/cfm/weather_data3.cfm/region=3_south_america_wmo_region_3/country=VEN/cname=Venezuela.

U.S. Energy Information Administration. "Residential Energy Consumption Survey (RECS)." Retrieved on June 2, 2012. http://www.eia.gov/consumption/residential/reports/electronics.cfm.

Valencia Ramírez, Christóbal. "Venezuela's Bolivarian Revolution: Who Are the Chavistas?" *Latin American Perspectives* 32, no. 3 (May 2005): 79–97. http://www.jstor.org/stable/30040243.

Velasco, Nancy. "200 familias invadieron torre bancaria de Fogade." *El Universal* (Caracas). October 21, 2007. http://www.eluniversal.com/2007/10/31/ccs_art_200-familias-invadie_567639.shtml.

———. "Se consolida invasión de la Torre de David tras dos años y medio." *El Universal* (Caracas). April 17, 2010. http://www.eluniversal.com/2010/04/17/ccs_art_se-consolida-invasio_1865816.shtml.

"Venezuela Buries Truckloads of Its Dead." *New York Times.* December 22, 1999. http://www.nytimes.com/1999/12/22/world/venezuela-buries-truckloads-of-its-dead.html.

"Venezuela Faces Serious Housing Crisis." *El Universal* (Caracas). February 4, 2011. http://www.eluniversal.com/2011/02/04/en_ing_esp_venezuela-faces-seri_04A5114691.shtml

"Venezuela Parliament Gives Hugo Chavez More Powers." *BBC.* December 18, 2010. http://www.bbc.co.uk/news/world-latin-america-12024935.

"Venezuela Toll in Floods and Slides Said to Exceed 5,000." *New York Times.* December 20, 1999. http://www.nytimes.com/1999/12/20/world/venezuela-toll-in-floods-and-slides-said-to-exceed-5000.html.

"Venezuelan Supreme Court Endorses Land Grabbing Alleging the Right to Food." *MercoPress.* December 17, 2011. http://en.mercopress.com/2011/12/17/venezuelan-supreme-court-endorses-land-grabbing-alleging-the-right-to-food.

Watson, Donald, Alan Plattus, and Robert Shibley. *Time-Saver Standards for Urban Design.* New York: McGraw-Hill, 2003.

"The Weakening of the 'Strong Bolívar.'" *The Economist.* January 14, 2010. http://www.economist.com/node/15287355.

Wieczorek, G.F., et al. "Debris-flow and Flooding Hazards Associated with the December 1999 Storm in Coastal Venezuela and Strategies for Mitigation." *U.S. Geological Survey.* http://pubs.usgs.gov/of/2001/ofr-01-0144/.

Wilpert, Gregory. "Chavez Presented Over 3,000 Titles as Part of Venezuela's Urban Land Reform." *venezuelanalysis.com.* October 25, 2004. http://venezuelanalysis.com/news/752.

———. "Venezuela's Quiet Housing Revolution: Urban Land Reform." *venezuelanalysis.com.* September 12, 2005. http://venezuelanalysis.com/analysis/1355.

Wilson, Peter. "The Skyscraper Slums of Caracas." *Foreign Policy.* January 6, 2012. http://www.foreignpolicy.com/articles/2012/01/06/skyscraper_slum_caracas.

IMAGE CREDITS

All images by Iwan Baan, with the exception
of the following:

Archivo Fotográfico Shell-CIC UCAB,
Universidad Catolíca Andrés Bello
Pages 74, 75

Inmuebles Magazine/Pineda y Lorenzo
Pages 90, 91, 92, 93, 132

SuAT
Pages 337, 338, 340, 341, 342, 343, 345, 348, 349

Thom Quine
Page 32

U-TT
Pages 80–81, 82–83, 84–85, 86, 97, 102–103, 104–105,
136, 137 (top), 142–143, 147, 165, 166, 167, 168, 169,
170, 171, 172, 173, 174, 175, 176–177, 179, 211, 218, 219,
224, 225, 236, 237, 238, 239, 240, 241, 242, 243, 368,
369, 370 (top), 378, 379, 380–381

U-TT/André Cypriano
Pages 366, 367

U-TT/Daniel Schwartz
Pages 137 (bottom), 139, 140, 146, 149 (top), 178, 208,
209, 210, 213, 215 (bottom), 216, 222, 364 (right)

U-TT/Erik-Jan Ouwerkerk
Page 364 (top left)

U-TT/Ilana Millner
Page 31

U-TT/Markus Kneer
Page 149 (bottom)

U-TT/Sabine Bitter and Helmut Weber
Page 364 (bottom left)

Yona Friedman
Pages 372, 373

BIOGRAPHIES

Iwan Baan

*1975 in Alkmaar, The Netherlands. Baan's photographs feature regularly in such journals as *Domus, A+U Magazine, Mark,* and *Abitare,* as well as the *New Yorker* and the *New York Times.* Interested especially in the effect of architecture on its surroundings, Baan incorporates the urban, social, and economic settings of the built environment into his stories. He has worked with such internationally recognized architects as Rem Koolhaas – OMA, Herzog & de Meuron, Toyo Ito, Steven Holl, and Zaha Hadid. Part of the team awarded the Golden Lion at the 13th International Architecture Exhibition – la Biennale di Venezia, for the "Torre David/Gran Horizonte" installation.

Alfredo Brillembourg

*1961 in New York, USA. Co-founder and co-principal of the interdisciplinary architecture and urban design firm, Urban-Think Tank. Brillembourg holds a Master of Science in Architectural Design (1986) from Columbia University's Graduate School of Architecture, Preservation, and Planning, and served as a guest professor at GSAPP from 2007–2010. In 2010 he was appointed co-Chair of Architecture and Urban Design, D-ARCH, ETH Zürich. Co-editor of *Informal City: Caracas Case* (2005), and co-founder of the Sustainable Living Urban Model (S.L.U.M. Lab). Part of the team awarded the Golden Lion at the 13th International Architecture Exhibition – la Biennale di Venezia, for the "Torre David/Gran Horizonte" installation.

Jimeno A. Fonseca

*1988 in Tunja, Colombia. Holds degrees in Civil Engineering (B.Sc. PUJ 2009) and Architectural Engineering with the highest honors (M.S.c. con Lode POLIMI 2011). Researcher of sustainable urban infrastructure systems at the professorship of Architecture and Sustainable Building Technologies (SuAT), ETH Zürich. Lives and works in Zürich.

André Kitagawa

*1973 in Sao Paulo, Brazil. Graduate from the Faculty of Architecture and Urbanism of the University of São Paulo (1999). As a comic artist and illustrator, Kitagawa has contributed to several periodicals and anthologies in Latin America. He also works as an animator, having made films for MTV Brazil. Kitagawa won the Piracicaba International Humor Exhibition in 2000 and the HQ Mix Award in 2003. He is the author of the graphic album Chapa Quente, which was adapted for film in 2005. Lives and works in São Paulo.

Hubert Klumpner

*1965 in Salzburg, Austria. Co-founder and co-principal of the interdisciplinary architecture and urban design firm, Urban-Think Tank. Klumpner holds a Master of Science in Architecture and Urban Design (1995) from Columbia University's Graduate School of Architecture, Preservation, and Planning, and served as a guest professor at GSAPP from 2007–2010. In 2010 he was appointed co-Chair of Architecture and Urban Design, D-ARCH, ETH Zürich. Co-editor of *Informal City: Caracas Case* (2005), and co-founder of the Sustainable Living Urban Model (S.L.U.M.) Lab. Part of the team awarded the Golden Lion at the 13th International Architecture Exhibition – la Biennale di Venezia, for the "Torre David/Gran Horizonte" installation.

Andres Lepik

*1961 in Augsburg, Germany. Professor for Architectural History and Curatorial Studies at TUM and Director of Architecture Museum München. From 2000 to 2007 he worked as Architecture Curator at Neue Nationalgalerie Berlin, and from 2007 to 2011 at The Museum of Modern Art where he presented "Small Scale, Big Change. New Architectures of Social Engagement" in 2010. Lives and works in Munich and Berlin.

Arno Schlueter

*1974 in Freiburg i.Br.,Germany, studied architecture at TU Karlsruhe (Dipl.Ing.) and information and building technologies at ETH Zürich (Dr.sc.ETH). Since 2010 he has served as Assistant Professor of Architecture & Sustainable Building Technologies. He is the co-founder and head of the board of Keoto AG, an ETH Spinoff for zero emissions architecture and engineering. Lives and works in Zurich.

Christian Schmid

*1958 in Zurich, Switzerland, studied geography and sociology. He is adjunct professor of sociology at the Department of Architecture at ETH Zürich and researcher at ETH Studio Basel/Contemporary City Institute. In 1991 he was cofounder of the International Network for Urban Research and Action (INURA). His writing and teaching focus on theories of space and urbanization, comparative urban studies, and urban social movements. He is the author of *Stadt, Raum und Gesellschaft: Henri Lefebvre und die Theorie der Produktion des Raumes* (Steiner 2005). Together with Roger Diener, Jacques Herzog, Marcel Meili, and Pierre de Meuron he has authored *Switzerland – an Urban Portrait* (Birkhauser 2005).

ACKNOWLEDGMENTS

The importance of the **Schindler Group**'s participation in the Torre David project cannot be overstated. Not only has their generous funding sustained our research: their unwavering commitment to our efforts sets a significant precedent for collaboration between first-world industry and third-world informal urban areas. We are especially grateful to Schindler's **Paul Friedli** and **Kilian Schuster,** for their close involvement throughout the project. It is our hope that other companies, of similar vision and dedication, will follow Schindler's example.

The support of the **ETH Zürich Department of Architecture** has been critical to the successful production of this book. As our host institution and research base, the ETH has provided invaluable support and fosters a culture of collaboration and curiosity that has enabled us to connect with many colleagues in our pursuit of truly interdisciplinary research. We would especially like to thank **Sacha Menz**, Dean of the Department of Architecture, for his support of our efforts.

Iwan Baan's collaboration and contribution were invaluable in documenting Torre David's remarkable reality and translating it onto the page. Iwan's photographic exploration blurs the boundary between architectural and documentary photography, revealing the structural complexities of the site as well as the vibrant community that its residents have created.

We are deeply grateful for the creative collaboration of **Lars Müller, Michael Ammann,** and **Martina Mullis,** of Lars Müller Publishers, whose patient guidance and enthusiasm made the realization of this book possible.

We extend our sincere thanks to our colleagues from the Institute of Technology in Architecture (ITA), ETH Zürich, **Arno Schlueter** and **Jimeno A. Fonseca,** for their valuable contributions to Chapter III and for the insight they provided on the future of sustainable technology in the developing world.

Andres Lepik and **Christian Schmid,** ETH Zürich, generously contributed their time and knowledge, framing this book with their broad and learned perspectives.

Urban-Think Tank draws on many sources and resources in our work. Our research on Venezuelan history was aided and informed by **Yvette Sanchez,** University St. Gallen; **Thomas Meister**; and **Gerson Revanales,** Universidad Central de Venezuela.

We are very appreciative of the support we received from **Yona Friedman,** a visionary whose work we have long admired and who welcomed us into his home to discuss Torre David. Yona has inspired U-TT since our earliest days, and his ideas continue to influence our research into and thinking about the new city.

David Brillembourg Jr. graciously agreed to an interview for this book. His reflections on his father's life and work provided important personal insight, as well as enlivened the history of Caracas' development and of Torre David.

Thank you to those who assisted and supported us in Caracas, among them **Clara Brillembourg, Reinaldo Di Fino, Luisa Virginia Gonzalez, Carlos Mendoza, Maria Los Ángeles Mendoza, Romains, Kai** and **Ana Luisa Rosenberg,** and **Maria Gabriela Sarmiento.**

Many thanks to **Enrique Gómez** and **Julio Rey** for their informative interview and for providing us with original project photographs and drawings. Additional thanks to **René Brillembourg** for his thoughtful reflections on the construction of Torre David.

We would especially like to acknowledge **Michael Contento, Rafael Machado, Ilana Millner,** and **Daniel Schwartz,** whose determination, persistence, and commitment to excellence played a vital role in seeing this book through to completion.

We owe an enormous debt of gratitude to the residents of Torre David, whose ingenuity and determination inspired us to explore and discover what lay behind the forbidding façade and daunting height. Our special thanks to **Gladys Flores** who gave us invaluable guidance and access into the inner workings of Torre David. Additional thanks to **Andrea, Lizbet de Ávila, Belica, Josue Ramón Centeno, Carmen Colmenares, Alexander "el Niño" Daza, Deivis, Fernando, Frankenstein, Grabiel, Jonkel, Ivan Morales, Jorge Morales, Yolanda Ramirez, Mariá Reyes, Ingrid Rodriguez, Tali,** and **Alfredo Zambrano.**

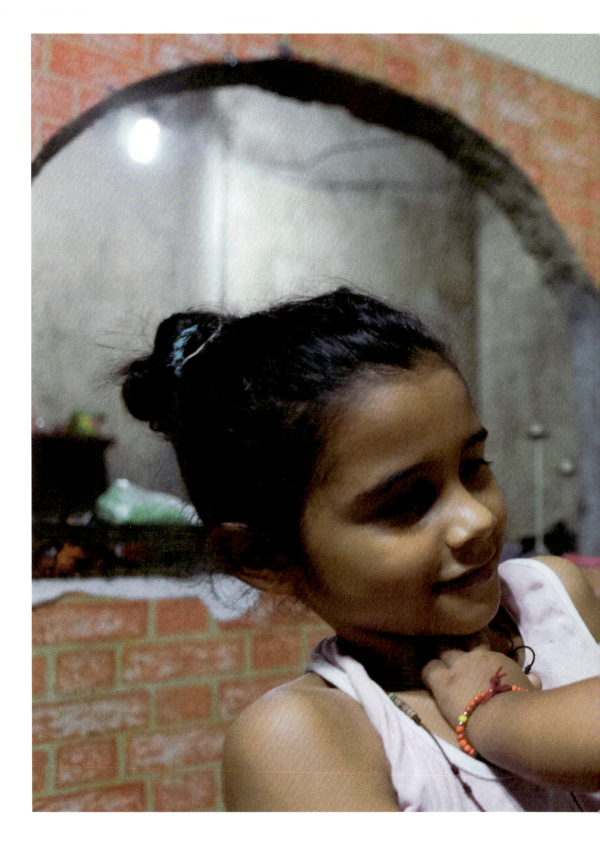

Tu Eres mi refugio Y m
Plaza Fuerte, mi Dios
en Quien De Veras
confiaré.
Salmo, 91:2

TORRE DAVID
INFORMAL VERTICAL COMMUNITIES

Urban-Think Tank
Chair of Architecture and Urban Design
ETH Zürich

Photographs by Iwan Baan

With contributions by:
Alfredo Brillembourg & Hubert Klumpner;
André Kitagawa (Graphic Novella); Andres Lepik
(Introduction); Christian Schmid (Afterword);
Arno Schlueter, Jimeno A. Fonseca, Architecture
and Sustainable Building Technologies (SuAT),
ETH Zürich (Chapter III Research, Data Analysis,
& Technical Graphics)

Project Directors:
Alfredo Brillembourg & Hubert Klumpner
Project Managers and Lead Researchers:
Michael Contento, Rafael Machado (Caracas)

Research Team: Joost deBont, Nicolas Matranga,
Ilana Millner, José Antonio Nuñez, Mathieu Quilici,
Daniel Schwartz, Lindsey Sherman
Conceptual Development Support: Markus Kneer,
Justin McGuirk
Draft Text: Ilana Millner, Daniel Schwartz
Copyediting and Revisions: Erika Rosenfeld
Author Support and Proofreading: Ilana Millner
Translations: Ishbel Flett (German-English),
Carolina Montilla (Spanish-English)

Graphics & 3D Renderings: Michael Contento, Susana
Garcia, Rafael Machado, Mathieu Quilici; Frederic
Schwarz & Kaspar Helfrich (BHS Architekten);
Anja Willmann (SuAT), Barnim Lemcke (SuAT)
Project Photography: Daniel Schwartz

Administrative Support: Flavia Reginato, Allison
Schwartz, Ramona Sorecau

Design: Integral Lars Müller/Lars Müller and Martina Mullis
Lithography: Ast & Fischer, Wabern, Switzerland
Printing and binding: Kösel, Altusried-Krugzell, Germany
This book was printed on eco-friendly paper:
Lessebo Design Smooth white, 150 g/m², supplied by
Geese Papier, Henstedt-Ulzburg/Germany. www.geese.de

Urban-Think Tank
Chair of Architecture and Urban Design
ETH Zürich
www.u-tt.arch.ethz.ch
www.u-tt.com

Lars Müller Publishers
Zürich, Switzerland
www.lars-mueller-publishers.com

ISBN 978-3-03778-298-9

Printed in Germany

Eidgenössische Technische Hochschule Zürich
Swiss Federal Institute of Technology Zurich

DARCH
Department of Architecture

Schindler